Double Standard
Abuse Scandals and the Attack on the Catholic Church

David F. Pierre, Jr.

Mattapoisett, Massachusetts USA

© 2010 by David F. Pierre, Jr.
www.themediareport.com
All rights reserved.

ISBN: 1453730699
EAN-13: 9781453730690

Printed in the United States of America.

Table of Contents

	Introduction	1
1	Failing Grades	7
2	Not the Catholic Church	15
3	Administrators, Not Bishops	29
4	Just One District	33
5	Trailblazing	43
6	Two Sides	53
7	The Voice of an Accused Priest	59
8	"Repressed Memories"?	67
9	SNAP and Friends	75
10	An ACORN in SNAP	81
11	No Good Deed …	93
12	Times Have Changed	99
13	Working the Pews	103
14	Attorney Jeff Anderson	109
15	"Considerable Doubt"	123
16	*Deliver Us From Evil*	129
17	Roman Polanski: Not a Catholic Priest	139
18	Silent Ambassadors	147
	Index	153
	Recommended by the Author	157

Introduction

It's not the media's fault.

The media didn't cause the abuse scandal of the Catholic Church. Priests and bishops acted wrongly, and they harmed children terribly. That's a plain fact.

Addressing a group of reporters on a plane flight to Portugal in May 2010, Pope Benedict XVI openly acknowledged that the "greatest persecution of the Church comes not from her enemies without, but arises from sin within the Church." He added, "The Church thus has a deep need to relearn penance, to accept purification, to learn forgiveness on the one hand, but also the need for justice. Forgiveness does not replace justice."[1]

The Holy Father is correct, of course. There are few crimes that revolt more than the sexual abuse of a child. Nothing justifies such an evil. Its harm to the victims is immeasurable. The faith of countless individuals has been shattered. The damage to the Church has been devastating.

Nevertheless, this reality of abuse by Catholic clergy is separate from the deep-rooted and pervasive unfairness that has characterized the coverage of the abuse scandals in the American media.

For example, because of several protective measures American bishops have implemented in recent years (see Chapters 5 and 11), it is seldom that a Catholic priest be contemporaneously charged with abusing a child. In the entire year of 2009 in the United States, credible and contemporaneous charges of abuse were filed against a total of six priests.[2] While even a total of six is six too many, the figure is indicative of an organization that has forcefully worked to rectify a serious problem.

Yet you'd never know it from the media coverage. Many would have you believe that uncontrollable priests are continually on the prowl to attack every child they can get their hands on. The image of the "pedophile priest" is now a mainstay in American culture, promulgated across the landscape in television, newspapers, radio, and the Internet.

In 2007, the Associated Press reported, "[They're] groped. They're raped. They're pursued [and] seduced."[3] But the AP wasn't talking about kids in the Catholic Church. They were talking about the widespread sexual abuse of innocent students happening today in our nation's public schools. Yet only five small newspapers carried the astonishing series by the AP.[4] While the focus on the Catholic Church never seems to cease, abuse and cover-ups in other segments of society have not garnered nearly the amount of attention that the Church has.

In addition, massive sex abuse lawsuits involving other organizations largely go unreported. In 2004, when more than 500 alleged victims of child sexual abuse sued the Hare Krishnas for more than $400 million, the media barely noticed. Lawyer David Liberman, who represented the Krishnas, said the lack of press coverage worked to the

Introduction

group's advantage when the organization filed for bankruptcy. Liberman told the *National Catholic Register*, "I was very pleased to be representing the Krishna Identity, and not the Catholic Church."[5]

Why the discrepancy in reporting? Does the awful abuse of children really bother the media, or is it troublesome to them only if the word "priest," "bishop," or "Cardinal" is in someone's job title?

Maybe the media sees something about the Catholic Church that it wishes to attack it.

Surely this is an issue worth exploring.

During the Lenten season of 2010, the *New York Times* released a towering front-page story with the provocative headline, "Vatican Declined to Defrock U.S. Priest Who Abused Boys."[6] Indeed, the story highlighted the atrocious case of a Milwaukee priest who had harmed scores of boys at a Wisconsin school for the deaf. The priest died in the 1988 and was last accused of abusing boys in 1974.

As Holy Week arrived, the media uncritically seized on the *Times* story. From the intensity of the coverage, one would have thought the abuse had only occurred a week earlier, not decades earlier. Hundreds of newspapers relayed the *Times*' report. And venues like ABC's *Good Morning America*, the *Boston Globe*, and HBO's *Real Time With Bill Maher* announced the message clearly: the Vatican had adamantly refused to discipline the abusive cleric.

There was one serious problem, however. The story was false. The piece, authored by Laurie Goodstein, went out of its way to try to implicate the current pontiff, Pope Benedict XVI, in allowing the abusive priest to stay in ministry. Had Goodstein taken the time to speak with Fr. Thomas Brundage, the Judicial Vicar in Milwaukee, who supervised the case of which she wrote, she would have discovered there is "no reason to believe that [the Pope] was involved at all" in the case.[7] The decisions about disciplining the abusive priest were made by Church officials here in the United States.

"Discerning truth takes time, and it is apparent that the *New York Times*, the Associated Press and others did not take the time to get the facts correct," added Brundage.[8]

Unfortunately, Ms. Goodstein relied on information supplied by Minnesota attorney Jeff Anderson, a professional litigant who has filed hundreds of lawsuits against the Catholic Church. Anderson had a vested interest in the case, as he was representing former students at the school for the deaf. Father Raymond J. de Souza at the *National Review* could not help but notice, "The appearance here is one of a coordinated campaign, rather than disinterested reporting."[9]

But the damage was done. In the eyes of the public, the Catholic Church remained an ancient cabal oblivious and insensitive to the crime of child abuse. One cannot help but wonder if that was the goal of the *Times* all along.

But shortly after Easter Sunday of 2010, former mayor of New York and U.S. Congressman Edward "Ed" Koch, a Jewish politician, noticed something. While acknowledging the "horrendous" crimes of abuse that were committed, "many of those in the media who are pounding on the Church and the pope today clearly do it with delight, and some with malice." He said the "continuing attacks" by the media on the Church and Pope Benedict XVI had become "manifestations of anti-Catholicism."[10]

Mr. Koch added, "Yes, terrible acts were committed by members of the Catholic clergy ... [but] it is trying desperately to atone for its past by its admissions and changes in procedures for dealing with pedophile priests." He concluded, "The Roman Catholic Church is a force for good in

Introduction

the world, not evil ... [T]he existence of 1 billion, 130 million Catholics worldwide is important to the peace and prosperity of the planet."[11]

Not surprisingly, not a single major American media outlet picked up on the remarks by Mr. Koch. In the same week that the *New York Times* completely ignored the notable remarks of its city's former mayor, it rather renewed the focus of its reporting by relaying allegations of abuse by about five Catholic clergy from the 1950's to the early 1990's – in *Norway*.

NOTES AND REFERENCES

1   "Interview of the Holy Father Benedict XVI with the Journalists on the Flight to Portugal," Papal Flight, May 11, 2010. Downloaded from http://www.vatican.va/holy_father/benedict_xvi/speeches/2010/may/documents/hf_ben-xvi_spe_20100511_portogallo-interview_en.html

2   Center for Applied Research in the Apostolate, "2009 Survey of Allegations and Costs: A Summary Report for the Secretariat of Child and Youth Protection, United States Conference of Catholic Bishops," Chapter Four, Georgetown University, Washington, D.C. February 2010.

3   Associated Press, "Sexual misconduct plagues U.S. schools: Survey finds 2,500 incidents over 5 years, across all types of districts," October 20, 2007. Downloaded from http://www.msnbc.msn.com/id/21392345/ns/us_news-education/

4   Catholic League for Religious and Civil Rights, "Media ignore sexual abuse in schools," press release, November 5, 2007. Downloaded from http://www.catholicleague.org/release.php?id=1354

5   Wayne Laugesen, "Abuse Crackdown Gives Some a Pass," *National Catholic Register*, July 9-15, 2006, p. 12.

DOUBLE STANDARD

[6] Laurie Goodstein, "Vatican Declined to Defrock U.S. Priest Who Abused Boys," *New York Times*, March 25, 2010, A1.

[7] Fr. Thomas Brundage, "Fr. Tom Brundage's Statement on Fr. Lawrence Murphy Case," Archdiocese of Milwaukee, April 1, 2010. Downloaded from http://www.archmil.org/News/Fr.TomBrundageSetstheRecordStr1.htm

[8] Ibid.

[9] Fr. Raymond J. de Souza, "A Response to the New York Times," *National Review Online*, March 27, 2010. Downloaded from http://corner.nationalreview.com/post/?q=ZDkxYmUzMTQ1YWUyMzRkMzg4Y2RiN2UyOWIzNDVkNDM=

[10] Zenit.org, "Ed Koch: Anti-Catholicism Evident in Media," April 12, 2010. Downloaded from http://www.zenit.org/article-28877?l=English

[11] Ibid.

1

Failing Grades

In writing about the Catholic Church abuse scandal for a May 2010 cover story in *Time* magazine, Jeff Israely and Howard Chua-Eoan asked, "Why didn't the church simply report to the civil authorities the crimes its priests were suspected of committing?" They then boldly claimed, "[N]owhere was there a more systemic tendency to cover up the shame and scandal than in Catholic parishes and orphanages ... which showed no compunction about avoiding the civil authorities altogether."[1]

SNAP, the Survivors Network of Those Abused by Priests, an outspoken advocacy group for clergy abuse victims, has also made the similar claim, "No other institution in the history of America has been afforded such extraordinary latitude to internally address its illegalities without legal intervention and sanction."[2]

But are these assertions actually *true*? Did the Church enjoy a unique privilege in systematically dodging authorities in cases of child abuse? Neither *Time* nor SNAP provided any sources for their claims.

DOUBLE STANDARD

To find the answer, one does not need to look further than the American public school system.

An important 2004 Department of Education report delivers valuable insight on this paramount issue. Authored by Hofstra University professor Charol Shakeshaft, *Educator Sexual Misconduct: A Synthesis of Existing Literature*[3] thoroughly examines the widespread problem of child sexual abuse by teachers in our nation's public schools.

In an explosive section discussing the consequences (or lack thereof) of known abusers, the report states, "In an early [1994] study of 225 cases of educator sexual abuse in New York, all of the accused had admitted to sexual abuse of a student but none of the abusers was reported to authorities."[4]

That is an important and alarming fact. Here's a visual of that startling statistic:

Number of abusive educators: **225**
Number reported to police: **0**

So, in other words, as recently as 1994, it was the *universal* practice in New York among school administrators not to call police to report abusers.

In addition, that same cited 1994 study, authored by Hofstra's Shakeshaft and Audrey Cohan, reported that only *1 percent* of those abusive educators lost their license. In addition, most amazingly, "25 percent received *no consequence* or were reprimanded informally and off-the-record. Nearly 39 percent chose to leave the district, *most with positive recommendations* or even retirement packages intact" (emphasis added).[5]

It's mind-blowing. A large percentage of abusive teachers got "positive recommendations," even though districts *knew* they had harmed children. If this were the

Failing Grades

Catholic Church doing this, the media would be screaming "cover-up." Yet you'd be hard pressed to find a journalist at any major newspaper bellowing about the clear and pervasive obscuration that's happened within the walls of our local schools. And if the 1994 study weren't convincing enough, four years later, in 1998, *Education Week* essentially confirmed Shakeshaft's and Cohan's findings. The newspaper published an eye-opening, multi-faceted, three-week study on educator misconduct in public schools. One of their articles chronicled the practice of "passing the trash," in which an abusive teacher goes from one school to another unscathed. The paper reported:

- "It is no secret in education circles that these itinerant abusers, often called 'mobile molesters,' are abetted by school officials who let them quietly slip away when allegations arise";
- "Facing the prospect of costly and risky court fights, some districts cut deals. Such agreements vary, but in many cases they entail keeping silent about accusations as long as an employee resigns";
- "Even if they don't reach explicit agreements to keep quiet, many school officials remain reluctant to pass along potentially damaging information about former employees – often at the urging of school lawyers"; and
- "When employees leave amid allegations of misconduct, some school officials don't just keep quiet. They sing the employees' praises in letters of reference designed to help them move on."[6]

DOUBLE STANDARD

A lot of this should sound familiar. It's exactly what the Church was known to do during the 1960's, 1970's, and early 1980's. But by the mid-1990's, as records now show, the Catholic Church in the United States had largely ceased such practices. (There are glaring exceptions, of course. The case of Paul Shanley in Boston would be one.)

But as *Education Week*, "American education's newspaper of record," revealed, as recently as 1998, it was "no secret" that schools shuffled known molesters around to different schools and cut secret deals with them. Calling the police wasn't even on the radar.

Have America's public schools routinely covered up child sex abuse by teachers? Absolutely, and studies clearly show this.

Now for the next question: Where has been the national media outrage?

A "pedophilia" crisis?

Probably the biggest misrepresentation of the Catholic clergy abuse scandal has been that the entire narrative has been a "pedophilia" crisis; that is, priests largely abused young girls and boys.

Here's the truth: In the general population, the clear majority of reported child sex abuse victims are female. Yet, as the expansive 2004 John Jay research study of Catholic clergy abuse reported, a whopping 81 percent of victims were *male*; only 19 percent of alleged victims were female.[7]

In addition, over 78 percent of victims were aged 11 years or older at the time of the alleged abuse, with over 27 percent being between the ages of 15 and 17.[8]

As pedophilia is defined as the sexual attraction to *prepubescent* children, what the statistics of the Catholic clergy scandal clearly show is that this was largely (although not exclusively, of course) a crisis of homosexual men preying on innocent teenage boys.

Journalists, liberal commentators, and victims' lawyers have strongly sought to deny the prominent role that homosexual priests have played in the Church abuse crisis. (California victim attorney John Manly has falsely claimed, "[The clergy abuse crisis] is not a problem with gay priests. That is a myth. It has nothing to do with homosexuality."[9])

A rare instance when the role of homosexuals was publicly acknowledged in a major forum was during a 2002 television segment on CNN. Discussing the Catholic clergy abuse scandal was the openly gay Al Rantel, who at the time was a popular radio talk show host on one of Los Angeles' largest stations, KABC.

"I don't say this happily ... because, as you may know, I happen to be gay myself. I'm openly gay here on the radio in Los Angeles, and have been for many years.

"But I have to tell you that, you know, even if you are gay, two and two is still four, and there's this proverbial 3,000-pound elephant sitting in the room that no one wants to talk about. This is not a pedophile issue, although the media called it a pedophile issue, because they don't want to insult the gay community. They don't want to be politically incorrect.

"But what you have here are not pedophiles. You have predatory gay men -- and there are some of us, believe me, I don't happen

to be one of them but there are some and we should all admit they're there. And these predatory gay men found their way into the Catholic priesthood in inordinately large numbers ... And these gay men have gone after young males. And I think it's disgraceful, and I think the media needs to address this. The gay community needs to address this."

(CNN Talkback Live, aired Friday, June 14, 2002[10])

Mr. Rantel is correct that the abuse was largely perpetrated by "predatory gay men." He also hit the nail on the head when he said that political correctness has played a damaging role in the reporting of the Catholic clergy scandals. Columnists do not want to upset the homosexual community by reporting gay men's prominent role in the these crimes.

Journalists owe it to the public to report stories fairly, accurately, and without bias.

Failing Grades

NOTES AND REFERENCES

[1] Jeff Israely and Howard Chua-Eoan, "The Trial of Pope Benedict XVI," *Time*, May 27, 2010.

[2] Survivors Network of Those Abused by Priests, "Sexual Abuse and the Catholic Church: The Need for Federal Intervention," November 2003 position paper. Downloaded from http://www.snapnetwork.org/Special_info/SNAP%20DOJ%20Position%20Paper.pdf

[3] Charol Shakeshaft (2004). *Educator Sexual Misconduct: A Synthesis of Existing Literature*, U.S. Department of Education.

[4] Ibid., citing Charol Shakeshaft and Audrey Cohan, (1994). *In loco parentis: Sexual abuse of students in schools. What administrators should know.* Report to the U.S. Department of Education, Field Initiated Grants.

[5] Ibid.

[6] Caroline Hendrie, "'Passing the Trash' by School Districts Frees Sexual Predators To Hunt Again," *Education Week*, December 9, 1998. (All four bulleted quotes are from this article.)

[7] John Jay College of Criminal Justice, "The Nature and Scope of the Problem of Sexual Abuse of Minors by Catholic Priests and Deacons in the United States," 2004. Available at http://www.usccb.org/nrb/

[8] Ibid.

[9] Interview from "Privacy Piracy," KUCI 88.9 FM, hosted by Mari Frank, guest John C. Manly, December 5, 2007.

[10] CNN, *CNN Talkback Live*, hosted by Arthel Neville, aired June 14, 2002. Transcript is at http://transcripts.cnn.com/TRANSCRIPTS/0206/14/tl.00.html

2

Not the Catholic Church

Is your child is safer in a public school than a Catholic Church? Don't count on it.

There's a lot more to that eye-opening 2004 Department of Education report. Harmonizing a number of large-sample studies of our nation's public schools, the author of the study, Dr. Charol Shakeshaft, concluded that "more than 4.5 million students are subject to sexual misconduct by an employee of a school sometime between kindergarten and 12th grade."[1] Startlingly, in the very next sentence she writes, "Possible limitations of the study would all suggest that the findings reported here *underestimate* educator sexual misconduct in schools"[2] (emphasis added). Shakeshaft also went on to add, "[A 2003 report] that nearly 9.6 percent of students are targets of educator sexual misconduct sometime during their school career presents the most accurate data available at this time."[3] There are roughly 50 millions students in America's public schools.

Dr. Shakeshaft has concluded that just between the years 1991 and 2000, United States educators sexually victimized 290,000 children.[4] (By contrast, a total of about 11,000 individuals allege abuse by Catholic clergy dating back to 1950.[5])

Most people would conclude that there is a grave and pervasive problem in our nation's schools when it comes to the sexual abuse of students by teachers. In addition, many people would think this problem would merit some serious media scrutiny.

But when Shakeshaft's blockbuster study was released, the media reaction was a collective yawn. Days after the study was released, a search of Google's comprehensive news archives returned only four publications reporting the study. Two of them were Catholic outlets. The *Christian Science Monitor* and the *Indianapolis Star* were the others, with both only making brief mentions of the report.[6] The *Star* buried news of the report in a larger story about – you guessed it – the Catholic Church abuse scandal.

The *Boston Globe*, the *New York Times*, and the *Los Angeles Times*, who have never shied from reporting just about every allegation of sexual misconduct by Catholic Church from anywhere in the world, no matter how long ago, did not find a single square inch to devote to the explosive study.

Three years later, in October 2007, the Associated Press published a stunning three-part series on sex abuse in public schools. After seven months of research it "found 2,570 educators whose teaching credentials were revoked, denied, surrendered or sanctioned from 2001 through 2005 following allegations of sexual misconduct."[7] Like the *Education Week* study eight years earlier (from Chapter 1), the series documented the widespread practice of "passing the trash." It also profiled the commonality of the "mobile molester."

Not the Catholic Church

Also included in the AP series was the sickening case of a teacher who kidnapped "more than 20 girls, some as young as 9. Among other things, he told prosecutors that he put rags in the girls' mouths, taped them shut and also bound their hands and feet with duct tape and rope for his own sexual stimulation."[8]

Not only did the AP chronicle a number of nauseating reports of abuse, it cataloged how the court system opposes victims who seek damages for the harm they have suffered. Unlike the Catholic Church, corporations, and other institutions, public schools have a special immunity from being sued in most abuse cases. Courts have ruled that unless a victim can prove that a school district undoubtedly *knew* that a teacher was a molester, there are no grounds for a lawsuit.

Pennsylvania sentenced a teacher to up to 31 years in state prison after it was discovered the educator repeatedly had sex with a 12-year-old girl, a student of his. The family filed a civil suit against the school district, but a federal judge dismissed the case, "saying administrators had no obligation to protect her from a predatory teacher since officials were unaware of the abuse, despite what the court called widespread 'unsubstantiated rumors' in the school."[9]

"The system fails hundreds of kids each year," the AP investigation concluded.[10]

Yet again, the American media was largely silent. Neither the *Boston Globe*, the *New York Times*, nor the *Los Angeles Times* touched the AP series.[11]

One can only wonder if the word "priest," "bishop," or "Cardinal" were in any of these stories, these papers would have acted otherwise.

In recent years there have been a number of eye-raising reports that catalog the awful sexual abuse by teachers and cover-ups by school districts. Notably, many of the investigations were conducted by lesser-known outlets, like the *Oregonian* and the *Seattle Times*. Some of the findings are simply outrageous. None of them were conducted by the *Boston Globe*:

- o Bombshell investigations by the *New York Post* in 2001 concluded, "At least one child is sexually abused by a school employee every day in New York City schools ... One-third of the employees accused of sex abuse are repeat offenders, who've already been cited for inappropriate behavior by school officials." The *Post* also found that the district had quietly forked over $18.7 million to victims in the previous five years.[12]
- o In June of 2002, the *New York Times* published an article, "Silently Shifting Teachers in Sex Abuse Cases." It reported, "When teachers are accused of sexual abuse, educators and law enforcement authorities say, districts often rid themselves of the problem by agreeing to keep quiet if the teacher moves on, sometimes even offering them a financial settlement. The practice, called passing the trash, avoids the difficulties of criminal prosecution or protracted disciplinary proceedings." The article then summarized a number of sickening cases around the country in which this exact practice happened.[13]
- o In February of 2004, the *Seattle Times* reported a case in which the Seattle School District actually wrote to a teacher, "[A] District investigation revealed that you went to the home of one of your female students at 3:00 a.m. on Sunday, January 22, 1995, you were let inside, and that you forced her to have sex with you." Not only did the district not call

the police, it allowed the man to resign and promised him it would not tell future employers about his crime.[14]
- The same *Seattle Times* report told the case of a teacher with *over two decades* of complaints in his file, some of which included groping and kissing young girls. "Yet he faced no punishment ... Instead of firing [the man], the district paid him the remainder of that year's salary, plus an additional $69,000, and promised to keep his record secret from future employers," the newspaper said. Needless to say, no one ran to call the police on this guy either.[15]
- A January 2007 investigation looked at the case of an Ohio school that hired a teacher largely because of a glowing letter of recommendation. (It highlighted his "outgoing personality" and proclaimed, "I wouldn't hesitate to hire him again.") The truth was that he had a disturbing and documented past which involved "too much touching of girls" and "taking girls into rooms with the door closed." The middle school teacher was later arrested for molesting a 14-year-old at his new job.[16]
- In 2007, the Southern California Inland Empire's *Daily Bulletin* reported the case of a substitute special education teacher who may have molested "**as many as 200 girls** over a three-year span, according to police."[17] The man had been allowed to work even though the California Commission on Teacher Credentialing sent him a letter of reprimand about his behavior.[18] In addition, he worked in 17 different school districts even though three districts banned him from teaching after suspicions of inappropriate conduct.[19] The man was eventually

sentenced to five years in prison on molestation charges.
- In 2007 and 2008, Central Illinois news outlets reported the case of a school giving a severance package and a bogus positive letter of recommendation to an elementary school teacher even though it had serious complaints against him. The man molested children at his new assignment, and he is now serving a 60-year sentence for molesting *10* second-grade girls.[20][21]
- In February of 2008, the *Oregonian* published a two-part series, of which one article was entitled, "Schools cut secret deals with abusive teachers." Among the paper's stunning findings: "During the past five years, nearly half of Oregon teachers disciplined for sexual misconduct with a child left their school districts with confidential agreements ... Some [districts and schools] promised cash settlements, health insurance and letters of recommendation as incentives for a resignation." The paper uncovered 47 such hush-hush arrangements, which allowed many abusive educators to keep on working.[22]
- In May of 2009, an explosive, front-page investigation in the *Los Angeles Times* reported that the Los Angeles Unified School District (LAUSD) "repeatedly" returned teachers and aides credibly accused of child molestation back to classrooms - and these individuals then molested children again. Among the cases: A district background check failed to pick up on a complaint that an applicant was under investigation by police for allegedly raping a 10-year-old boy repeatedly at a group home where he had worked. Within a week of a jury acquitting him, the

- district assigned the man to an elementary school to be a special education aide to a female second-grader.[23]
- In February of 2010, the *New York Post* reported the case of a New York City math teacher. At the beginning of his 32-year teaching career, the teacher impregnated and married a 16-year-old girl he had met when she was a 13-year-old student in junior high. In subsequent years, he also molested two 12-year-olds and another student. Yet he continued to collect a taxpayer-funded salary of $94,154 a year.[24]
- In March of 2010, the conservative web site *WorldNetDaily* published, "The big list: Female teachers with students." It exhaustedly combed the internet for underage sex crimes featuring only *female* educators. It chronicled a mind-blowing 231 cases from just the previous few years. All but two of the cases they posted happened since 2004, and only a single case was from outside the United States. (They inexplicably posted a case from Australia.)[25] One can only guess how many hundreds of other cases have never publicly surfaced or were quietly handled privately.

One of the leading experts on the subject of clergy sex abuse is Pennsylvania State University humanities professor Philip Jenkins. (In 1996, six years before the scandal exploded in America, Jenkins wrote a thoroughly researched book on the topic, *Pedophiles and Priests*.) In a June 2010 article for *USA Today*, Jenkins wrote, "If anyone believes that [Catholic] priests offend at a higher rate than teachers or non-celibate clergy, then they should produce the evidence on which they are basing that conclusion. I know of none."[26]

DOUBLE STANDARD

Another factor to note is that these awful cases of child sex abuse in schools are *all* quite recent. These are not enents from decades ago, when the vast majority of abuse by Catholic clergy is chronicled to have taken place. Abuse and cover-ups are happening *today* in our nation's public schools on a massive scale.

Just in the 2002 calendar year alone, the *Boston Globe* published an astonishing 947 items on the Catholic Church abuse scandal. Nine hundred forty-seven items in one year. Think about that. That is an average of over two-and-a-half items *per day*. Several of the cases that the paper chronicled dated back decades.

But where has the *Globe* been on the issue of sex abuse in public schools? Are we to believe that Boston Public Schools has a pristine record for the past several decades when it comes to handling cases of abuse? Years after its year-long "Spotlight Team" investigation into abuse in the Catholic Church, the paper hasn't seemed very interested in exerting the same resources into looking into abuse in any other institutions.

Not the Catholic Church

A celibacy problem?
A "Catholic" problem?

An oft-heard proclamation is that a major cause of the abuse crisis has been the mandatory vow of celibacy for Catholic priests. Individuals claim that the "unnatural" adherence to this practice causes priests to seek "release" by preying on innocent children.

Besides being a major insult to the millions of men through the centuries who have faithfully kept their vows, the assertion is not supported by data.

There is simply no evidence *at all* that Catholic clergy have offended at a higher rate than other religious denominations, where there are no celibacy requirements.

Although this fact has been reported in a number of places, an April 2010 article for *Newsweek* magazine (of all places) is quite helpful. It reported:

... "[B]ased on the surveys and studies conducted by different denominations over the past 30 years, experts who study child abuse say they see little reason to conclude that sexual abuse is mostly a Catholic issue";

... "Since the mid-1980s, insurance companies have offered sexual misconduct coverage as a rider on liability insurance, and their own studies indicate that Catholic churches are not higher risk than other congregations"; and

... "Insurance companies that cover all denominations ... [do] not charge Catholic churches higher premiums. 'We don't see vast difference in the incidence rate between one denomination and another,' says [an insurance company vice president]. 'It's pretty even across the denominations.' It's been that way for decades."[27]

Meanwhile, a little-known 2002 article in the *Christian Science Monitor* is sure to raise eyebrows. It reported the findings of surveys conducted by Christian Ministry Resources (CMR), a group that provides tax and legal advice to more than 75,000 Protestant congregations and 1,000 denominational agencies.

Monitor staffer Mark Clayton reported, "CMR's annual surveys of about 1,000 churches nationwide have asked about sexual abuse since 1993 ... The surveys suggest that over the past decade, the pace of child-abuse allegations against American churches has averaged 70 a week."[28]

70 child-abuse allegations *per week*? But wait. "[T]he 70 allegations-per-week figure actually could be higher, because underreporting is common."[29] Whoa.

"The Catholics have gotten all the attention from the media, but this problem is even greater with the Protestant churches simply because of their far larger numbers," James Cobble, executive director of CMR, told the *Monitor*.[30]

In October of 2009, the *New York Times* profiled the dark secrets of an Orthodox Jewish community in Brooklyn. It chronicled how members handled child-abuse complaints internally for decades by way of rabbinical courts. Even if they found a member guilty of the crime, they did not call secular authorities.[31] "Cover-up"? Definitely.

The article quoted an attorney representing the community, who said law enforcement should respect "religious sensitivities" when proceeding with the cases.

The *Times*' hair-raising article caught the attention - and ire - of the Catholic League for Religious and Civil Rights and its president Bill Donohue. "Allow a Catholic attorney to advise ['religious sensitivities'] and it's called corruption."[32]

In his statement about the article, Dr. Donohue continued, "Last year (2008), 40 minors in this small Jewish community said they were abused. Last year (2008), there were 10 such allegations in the entire Catholic Church in all 50 states. Catholics are fed up with the duplicity ... The politics of child rape is sickening."[33] Donohue is correct. And as those who have studied the issue have asserted, there has *never* been any evidence to show that Catholic priests have offended at a higher rate than teachers or non-celibate clergy.[34]

Here is another case in which the media has done a big disservice to the public.

NOTES AND REFERENCES

[1] Charol Shakeshaft (2004). *Educator Sexual Misconduct: A Synthesis of Existing Literature*, U.S. Department of Education.

[2] Ibid.

[3] Ibid.

[4] George Weigel, "Church gets an unfair rap: Pope has been at forefront of change," *Philadelphia Inquirer*, April 4, 2010.

[5] John Jay College of Criminal Justice, "The Nature and Scope of the Problem of Sexual Abuse of Minors by Catholic Priests and Deacons in the United States," 2004. Available at http://www.usccb.org/nrb/

[6] Jon E. Dougherty, "Sex Abuse by Teachers Said Worse Than Catholic Church," *Newsmax*, April 5, 2004. Downloaded from http://archive.newsmax.com/archives/articles/2004/4/5/01552.shtml

[7] Associated Press, "Sexual misconduct plagues U.S. schools."

[8] Ibid.

[9] Ibid.

[10] Ibid.

[11] Catholic League for Religious and Civil Rights, "Media ignore sexual abuse in schools."

[12] Douglas Montero, "Secret shame of our schools: Sexual abuse of students runs rampant," *New York Post*, July 30, 2001.

[13] Diana Jean Schemo, "Silently shifting teachers in sex abuse cases," *New York Times*, June 18, 2002.

[14] Maureen O'Hagan, "Teacher conduct proposal may get diluted," *Seattle Times*, February 23, 2004.

[15] Ibid.

[16] Michael Crowley, "Outrageous! Protect Our Kids! How is it that sexual predators are getting a free pass in our children's schools?" *Readers' Digest*, January 2007.

[17] Edward Barrera and Caroline An, "Allegations first lodged in '05," *Daily Bulletin* (CA), August 7, 2006.

[18] Wendy Leung and Edward Barrera, "Two districts failed to report accused molester's actions," *Daily Bulletin* (CA), August 10, 2006.

Not the Catholic Church

[19] Rod Leveque, "Parents seeking to sue districts over Olsen," *Daily Bulletin* (CA), February 23, 2007.

[20] Phyllis Coulter, "In '05, White agreed to resign with a letter of recommendation," *Pantagraph*, April 5, 2008.

[21] Edith Brady-Lunny, "White sentenced to 48 years for sex abuse in Urbana," *Pantagraph*, April 4, 2008.

[22] Amy Hsuan, Melissa Navas, and Bill Graves, "Schools cut secret deals with abusive teachers," *The Oregonian*, February 18, 2008.

[23] Jason Song, "Accused of sexual abuse, but back in the classroom," *Los Angeles Times*, May 10, 2009.

[24] Susan Edelman, Kathianne Boniello, and Cynthia R. Fagen, "Exiled Queens teacher on payroll despite knocking up student, *New York Post*, February 9, 2010.

[25] "The big list: Female teachers with students," *WorldNetDaily*, posted March 10, 2010 at http://www.wnd.com/index.php?fa=PAGE.view&pageId=39783

[26] Philip Jenkins, "How serious is the 'predator priest' problem?" *USA Today*, June 6, 2010.

[27] Pat Wingert, "Mean Men," *Newsweek*, April 8, 2010.

[28] Mark Clayton, "Sex abuse spans spectrum of churches," *Christian Science Monitor*, April 5, 2002.

[29] Ibid.

[30] Ibid.

[31] Paul Vitello, "Orthodox Jews Rely More on Sex Abuse Prosecution," *New York Times*, October 14, 2009, A1.

[32] Press release from The Catholic League For Religious and Civil Rights, "The Politics of Child Rape," October 14, 2009. From http://www.catholicleague.org/release.php?id=1693

DOUBLE STANDARD

[33] Ibid.

[34] Jenkins.

3

Administrators, Not Bishops

While the media continues to thrash Church officials for not reporting child abuse decades ago, consider what has been happening far more recently in just *one* of our nation's school districts, the Los Angeles Unified School District (LAUSD).

On May 1, 2008, police in South Gate, California, arrested Jesus I. Angulo, 35, and Maria Sotomayor, 36, the principal and vice-principal, respectively, at South East High School. Months earlier, a 13-year-old girl at the Los Angeles-area school came to them to report that the school's girls' soccer coach and substitute teacher, Jesus Salvador Saenz, had sex with her. By law the two administrators were required to immediately notify police or call the Los Angeles County Department of Children and Family Services. They did neither.

LAUSD is the nation's second largest school district. In 2007, Angulo took home a taxpayer-funded salary of $116,491.92 plus benefits; Sotomayor scored $86,266.08 plus benefits.[1]

DOUBLE STANDARD

How did LAUSD discipline the two administrators for breaking state law, shielding an alleged abuser, and failing to report suspected child abuse? Well, only eight days after they were arrested, the district returned the pair back to work. The Superintendent of LAUSD, Admiral David Brewer III, defended his decision by saying he wanted to "avoid disruptions"[2] with upcoming state academic testing and graduation activities.

A few months later, in September, Mr. Angulo pleaded "no contest" on one count of failing to report child abuse. Although the court could have sentenced him to six months in jail with a $1000 fine, a commissioner sentenced him to two years of probation and 100 hours of community service.[3]

In November, Ms. Sotomayor pleaded guilty to the same charge. The same commissioner sentenced her to one year of probation and 100 hours of community service.[4]

If you think LAUSD finally terminated the pair's employment after their sentences, think again.

Even after pleading "no contest" and guilty, the two administrators still enjoy full employment with LAUSD today. In fact, LAUSD has since given each administrator a promotion. Angulo has moved up to become Director of Student Services at Local District 5 in LAUSD. Sotomayor is now principal at South East High, having replaced Angulo.

In all the time since Angulo and Sotomayor were sentenced in court for their crimes and returned to work, not a single journalist has taken note. Again, if this were Los Angeles Cardinal Roger Mahony returning two *bishops* or *priests* who had been sentenced, you can surely bet there would be nothing short of a raging inferno in the Los Angeles media that would likely garner national attention.

Double standard, indeed.

Administrators, Not Bishops

NOTES AND REFERENCES

[1] In September of 2008, the Los Angeles *Daily News* obtained the LAUSD 2007 salary database through the California Public Records Act and posted it. The searchable database is at http://lang.dailynews.com/socal/lausdpayroll/

[2] Richard Winton and Howard Blume, "Charged pair back at school," *Los Angeles Times*, May 13, 2008, B1.

[3] "LAUSD Administrator Pleads in Child Abuse Case," Los Angeles County District Attorney's Office, September 3, 2008. http://da.lacounty.gov/mr/archive/2008/090308c.htm

[4] "LAUSD Administrator Pleads Guilty in Child Abuse Case," Los Angeles County District Attorney's Office, November 3, 2008. http://da.lacounty.gov/mr/archive/2008/110308a.htm

4

Just One District

As egregious as the incident at South East High School was, the case of assistant principal Steven Thomas Rooney will surely shock. In February of 2007, Los Angeles police arrested Rooney, 38, who was working as an assistant principal at Fremont High School in the Watts area of South Los Angeles. A stepparent had gone to question Rooney after he suspected that Rooney was having a sexual relationship with his 16-year-old stepdaughter.

An altercation between Rooney and the stepparent ensued, and Rooney reportedly pulled a gun on the parent. The teenager's family says that they complained to police, and the police began investigating Rooney's relationship with the underage girl.

It was not the first time that Mr. Rooney had shown disturbing and aggressive behavior. During a dispute at Fremont, he reportedly shoved another administrator, a dean. The teachers' union actually filed a grievance against Rooney for pushing the dean, but nothing resulted from it.[1]

In February 2007, the Los Angeles Unified School District (LAUSD) issued a confidential memo to district administrators about Rooney's arrest. The memo clearly stated:

> "[Los Angeles police are] investigating allegations that he had an unlawful sexual relationship with a minor."[2]

"An unlawful sexual relationship with a minor." With such a troubling record on their hands, common sense would dictate that officials at LAUSD would have motioned to terminate their working relationship with Rooney. Unfortunately, common sense was absent at LAUSD.

Amazingly, within six months, in August 2007, LAUSD reassigned Rooney to another school. This time LAUSD assigned him to the troubled Markham Middle School, also in South Los Angeles.

And within six months of serving at his new job, on March 4, 2008, Los Angeles police arrested Steve Rooney again. He had brazenly kidnapped and sexually attacked a 13-year-old Markham student, who was also a recent immigrant from El Salvador. Rooney abducted the girl outside a fast-food restaurant, forced her into his car, drove her to his downtown apartment, and raped her. Police booked Rooney on one felony count of kidnapping and two felony counts of aggravated sexual assault of a child. A judge set bail at $1 million.[3]

Los Angeles police investigated Rooney further, and within weeks, they charged Rooney with molesting yet another student at Markham, this one a 14-year-old girl.

The entire narrative is astonishing. By placing him back into an environment with children, LAUSD enabled Mr. Rooney to continue to prey on young girls. Even though they had received a memo that clearly stated that police were investigating Rooney for illegal sex with a minor, they reassigned him anyway without doing their own investigation.

Fox 11 television in Los Angeles looked into the case. They obtained copies of police search warrants from the investigation into Rooney's original 2007 arrest. Fox 11's John Schwada reported that the warrants revealed that an underage girl "admitted to a detective that she had been sexually involved with Rooney for a year." When police went to search Rooney's downtown apartment, detectives reportedly "found a photo of the [former] student and three vibrators, all on the nightstand next to Rooney's bed."[4]

Schwada also added this stunner: "The LAPD detective who supervised the case said Rooney's bosses at the school district were totally kept informed of their investigation."[5]

If the subject matter of the story weren't so shocking, an interview exchange that Schwada had with a lowly district official would be comical.

> FOX 11's SCHWADA: Did the LAUSD not look into [Rooney's previous arrest]?
> LAUSD OFFICIAL: Uh, I believe that's why we are calling this, uh, confidential investigation that is internal to the district itself.[6]

Did anyone get that?

The Superintendent of LAUSD during this time was Admiral David L. Brewer III. Even though he had no leadership experience in education, the District had hired Brewer for its top position in November of 2006 at an annual salary of $250,000 plus many perks and benefits. The February 2007 district memo that reported Mr. Rooney's original arrest was directly addressed to Admiral Brewer. Brewer should thank his lucky stars he is not a Catholic clergy. While Los Angeles media continue to hammer Cardinal Mahony for mistakes he made in the 1980's, not a single journalist called for Brewer's resignation in the face of the scandal. (By the end of 2008, everyone could see that Brewer was in a position that was way over his head. Again, he came to the job with no experience in education. The LAUSD school board ended its four-year agreement with the admiral, and Brewer walked away with a severance package estimated at a cool $500,000.[7])

Then there was the local district superintendent, Carol Truscott, who was an administrator directly responsible for reassigning Rooney to the school where he raped again. LAUSD allowed Truscott to continue in her taxpayer-funded job at over $170,000 a year plus benefits.[8]

In fact, there were a total of *eleven* LAUSD officials who received the memo clearly stating that Rooney was under investigation for illegal underage sex. Not a single one of these individuals lost their position.[9]

Placing Steve Rooney back into a school with children was callous enough. Then LAUSD allowed several administrators to keep their cushy positions. Yet the insensitivity did not end there.

> … When KNX radio reporter Charles Feldman questioned LAUSD Deputy Superintendent Ramon Cortines over the phone about the Rooney incident and other reports of abuse at LAUSD, Cortines became agitated by the questions and abruptly hung up on Feldman. (Along with Schwada, Charles Feldman was one of the few reporters in Los Angeles who really delved into this Rooney/LAUSD story.)[10]
>
> … When questioned on television about the Rooney incident, Cortines defiantly responded, "This is not

Just One District

out of the ordinary for school districts all over the nation. These things happen."[11]

... In a public statement about the Rooney affair, LAUSD falsely claimed that Los Angles police had not fully notified them about their investigation of Rooney for underage sex.[12]

Imagine the uproar if Catholic Church officials had reacted in the same defiant and dismissive ways that LAUSD officials did. Surely the media would have spotlighted an agitated "Cardinal Cortines" getting angry and hanging up the phone on a reporter.

Instead, criticism of LAUSD officials was sparse.

The Rooney affair and the arrests of the two administrators at South East High were not just isolated incidents in the 2008 year for LAUSD. An alarming number of other frightful cases were reported. The following incidents were documented during a mere *six-month* period in the one school district in 2008:

> ... Police charged a high school athletic coach with 12 felony counts of sexually assaulting an underage girl, including "five counts of sexual penetration with a foreign object while the victim was unconscious and one count of possession of child pornography." "[P]olice said they believe there may be other victims." The man was also a special education assistant;[13]
>
> ... A court sentenced a former Special Education high school teacher to three years in prison after charges of lewd conduct, child molestation, and abuse. The alleged crimes involved four of his "particularly vulnerable" students;[14]

… Police charged a special education aide for the district "already accused of videotaping himself molesting teenage girls in his private basketball program" with "having sexual contact with four more, including one who says he took her to a local hotel room for a weekend of sex";[15]

… Law enforcement arrested a high school principal for possessing child pornography on his home computer. Authorities also discovered that he "had posed as a 12-year-old girl in an online chat room and engaged in sexually explicit talk";[16]

… The FBI arrested a middle school special education teacher at his home on suspicion of possession of child pornography. An FBI spokeswoman said thousands of images of children were found on the man's computer, many of them pornographic. The FBI said it had learned the teacher was a subscriber to a child pornography website;[17]

… A high school teacher pleaded guilty and was sentenced to six months in jail for having sex with a minor. County deputies had found the teacher and the underage female student in the back seat of a car in a parking lot;[18]

… Police arrested a band teacher on charges of possessing child pornography on his laptop computer;[19]

… The district dismissed a high school girls' volleyball coach after a lawsuit surfaced alleging he had a sexual relationship with a female student at his previous school;[20]

… A jury awarded almost $1.6 million to three girls who were molested by an elementary school aide. The girls were ages 5 to 7 at the time of the assaults. The man is now serving 15 years to life in prison;[21]

Just One District

... KNX 1070 Newsradio in Los Angeles reported that 21 teachers and administrators had been yanked from schools just in previous months because of allegations of inappropriate sexual contact with kids;[22]

... A short time later, the *Los Angeles Times* then reported that "75 current employees are on hold in 'non-school' positions pending investigations into alleged inappropriate conduct."[23]

"*21* teachers and administrators"? "*75* current employees"? Who knows what the real number actually is. However, if this had been 21 or 75 "priests and bishops," one could safely bet that every news journalist in Los Angeles, along with members from SNAP, would be screaming about a "massive cover-up" and aggressively demanding the release of the names of every one of those priests and bishops. As it stood in this case, not a single media figure put forward this demand for LAUSD.

When studying the issue of teacher misconduct, one cannot help but wonder how many cases of abuse are quietly brushed "under the rug" and away from police and media attention.

Anonymous comments on the Internet should always be taken with a big grain of salt, but sometimes something rings all too true. In a discussion forum about an LAUSD case, a random member (who likely was not even from Los Angeles) posted the following comment:

> "We had a gym teacher at my school named Mr. Cox who we always suspected of doing shady things with the girls. They were always in his 'office' with the door closed. He resigned out of nowhere one day. The school

DOUBLE STANDARD

really did a good job of keeping that hushed up. I heard he bought a girl a laptop in exchange for sex."[24]

It makes you wonder. How often do incidents like these happen?

NOTES AND REFERENCES

[1] Tibby Rothman, "LAUSD's Markham asst. principal scandal," *LA Weekly*, March 27, 2008.

[2] "Isaacs Memo" posted by the *Los Angeles Times* in April of 2008.

[3] Andrew Blankstein and Howard Blume, "Educator arrested in sex case," *Los Angeles Times*, March 5, 2008. Also, Richard Winton, Andrew Blankstein and Howard Blume, "L.A. educator in sex case faced earlier investigation," *Los Angeles Times*, March 13, 2008.

[4] John Schwada, "Fox 11 Ten O'Clock News," Fox 11 Television, Los Angeles, March 11, 2008.

[5] Ibid.

[6] Ibid.

[7] Howard Blume, "David Brewer close to LAUSD exit deal, sources say," http://latimesblogs.latimes.com/lanow/2008/12/embattled-la-sc.html, December 8, 2008.

[8] Salary is from the Los Angeles *Daily News* LAUSD 2007 salary database at http://lang.dailynews.com/socal/lausdpayroll/ . Truscott retired in June 2009.

[9] In the entire LAUSD-Rooney affair, there appears to be *one* employee who was criminally charged and dismissed from LAUSD. It was a dean at Rooney's 2007 school, Foshay Learning Center. Alan Hubbard was charged with concealing evidence showing an affair between Rooney and an underage girl. Howard Blume, "Ex-L.A. dean sentenced for hiding evidence against

Just One District

teacher," *Los Angeles Times*, October 7, 2008. (Hubbard's name is not on the 2007 memo, however.)

[10] Charles Feldman, "21 LAUSD Employees Linked to Sex Abuse Claims," KNX 1070 radio, Los Angeles, March 2008.

[11] KNBC Television, Los Angeles. http://www.knbc.com/news/16267584/detail.html, March 2008.

[12] "Statement regarding LAUSD incident of employee misconduct: Ray Cortines, Senior Deputy Superintendent," May 2008. Downloaded from http://www.latimes.com/media/acrobat/2008-05/38573788.pdf

[13] Andrew Blankstein and Victoria Kim, "Dean held in Rooney molest case," *Los Angeles Times*, June 13, 2008.

[14] Associated Press, "Ex-Special education teacher sentenced in sex case," *Los Angeles Times*, May 22, 2008.

[15] Brandon Lowrey, "More girls accuse Birmingham High School ex-coach of sex allegations," *Daily News* (Los Angeles), October 18, 2008.

[16] Victoria Kim, "Principal posed as girl online, police say," *Los Angeles Times*, July 4, 2008.

[17] Andrew Blankstein, "Teacher arrested in child porn case," *Los Angeles Times*, April 10, 2008.

[18] Ari B. Bloomekatz, "Girl's ex-teacher going to jail," *Los Angeles Times*, August 27, 2008.

[19] Andrew Blankstein and Jason Song, "Foshay band teacher charged with possession of child porn," *Los Angeles Times*, June 6, 2008.

[20] Richard Winton, "Disclosure of sex abuse suit prompts firing," *Los Angeles Times*, July 8, 2008.

[21] Jason Song, "Jury awards nearly $1.6 million to 3 girls molested by former L.A. school aide," *Los Angeles Times*, October 22, 2008.

[22] Charles Feldman, "21 LAUSD Employees Linked to Sex Abuse Claims," KNX 1070 radio, Los Angeles, March 2008.

[23] Howard Blume, "2 removed in school sex cases," *Los Angeles Times*, May 8, 2008.

[24] Game-Spot Forums, "Off-Topic Discussion," comment posted on May 2, 2008, at http://www.gamespot.com/pages/forums/show_msgs.php?topic_id=26372265

Trailblazing

> "Whether the victim is a kidnapped sex slave in Thailand, a trafficked child camel jockey in the Persian Gulf states, or a fifth grader assaulted in an American elementary school, the fact that children and young people throughout the world are regularly subjected to sexual and physical abuse is a horror that ought to shock the conscience of humanity." – Theologian George Weigel, April 2010[1]

When it comes to resolving the issue of sex abuse by Catholic clergy, all people of good will want the same outcomes: *justice*, the *healing of victims*, and the *protection of children*.

But if these goals are to move towards fulfillment, we must clear the air of falsehoods, personal attacks, and unfair disparagement. They do nothing to advance towards the desired goals.

The Honorable Patrick J. Schiltz is a United States District Judge working in Minnesota. In his distinguished and extensive career in law, he has first-hand experience with over 500 abuse cases involving clergy of all denominations. He has spent "hundreds of hours" speaking with victims of abuse,[2] and his disgust with the sickening crime is truly palpable.

"I take a back seat to no one in my loathing of clergy sexual abuse," Schiltz has written.[3] By no means is the jurist an apologist for priests who wrecked immeasurable harm and the bishops who failed to halt it.

With that said, Judge Schiltz has aired his frustration over the fact the media has insisted in reporting the same overall narrative over and over again in its coverage of Catholic Church clergy abuse. In a series of articles for *Commonweal* Magazine, Schiltz wrote:

> I have challenged reporters to cite a single major element of the clergy sexual-abuse story that was not widely reported a decade ago. No reporter has been able to do so. I have also challenged reporters to cite another instance in the history of American journalism in which the press gave front-page coverage — not for a day or two, but for months on end — to a story that had been thoroughly covered a decade earlier. Again, no reporter has been able to do so.[4]

Here's the surprise. Schiltz did not write this in 2010, but in *2003*. One can only imagine that he was shaking his head in disbelief at the new tsunami of coverage seven years later in 2010.

Judge Schiltz is correct. If you pick up a copy of the *Boston Globe*, the *New York Times*, or the *Los Angeles Times*, and read about a case of abuse by Catholic Church clergy, the allegation being reported will almost *always* involve an episode from decades ago. And with the exception

Trailblazing

of the names being different, there is almost no new angle or element that differentiates it from any other case of reported clergy abuse.

Yet the media has insisted in "piling on" over cases of decades-old allegations.

In 2004, the John Jay College of Criminal Justice released a very important study, "The Nature and Scope of the Problem of Sexual Abuse of Minors by Catholic Priests and Deacons in the United States." It exhaustively combed through Catholic Church abuse data from 1950 to 2002. Although the study was commissioned by the United States bishops, the study was independently conducted. Many have praised its thoroughness, and no one has seriously challenged its findings.

The John Jay study is a sobering body of information. There are a few findings, however, which may surprise many observers, because the media have rarely, if ever, reported them:

- 149 priests, about 3 percent of all accused priests (or *one-tenth of one percent* of all priests who served in the United States from 1950 to 2002), account for a whopping 26% of all incidents of abuse. (These 149 are alleged to have abused 10 or more individuals.)
- The majority of all accused priests have just a single allegation.
- "Half of all allegations were made between ten and thirty years after the incident ... 25% were reported more than 30 years after the incident." "When all allegations are considered, only one in four allegations was made within ten years of the incident."

o The greatest incidence of abuse occurred between the mid-1960's and the early 1980's. Allegations of abuse by Catholic priests occurring since 1990 are seldom.[5]

Meanwhile, the Center of Applied Research in the Apostolate (CARA) has been continuing to track abuse data for the United States bishops. How many *new* accusations of abuse actually involve a person under the age of 18 *at the time of the allegation*? Here are the numbers of such cases reported separately each year from 2005 to 2009:

Year	Number of allegations involving a minor[6]
2009	6
2008	10
2007	4
2006	14
2005	9

Contrast the numbers above with the fact that, according to the authoritative John Jay study, 10,667 individuals made abuse allegations against 4,392 priests between 1950 and 2002.[7]

The above statistics need to be considered when viewers tune into their national or local newscast and hear reporters and lawyers conversing about abuse in the Catholic Church. Audiences need to ask themselves, "When is the abuse alleged to have occurred?"

"Give credit where credit is due." It's an old adage, but one is hard-pressed to see it applied to the Catholic Church.

While even a single case is disturbing, for an organization of nearly 70 million people, the evidence reveals that the Catholic Church has worked aggressively to combat child sexual abuse.

There's a reason that reported instances of abuse began to decline in the mid-1980's.

"As early as 1982, we saw policies and procedures coming to the attention of the USCCB (the United States Conference of Catholic Bishops) regarding specific child molestation cases," Teresa Kettelkamp, executive director of the Secretariat of Child and Youth Protection for the USCCB, told Tim Drake at the *National Catholic Register* in April 2010. "By 1983, 157 dioceses had policies in place."[8]

These policies later formulated the "Five Principles" in dealing with allegations of abuse. Bishops first articulated them in 1987 and then publicly pronounced them in 1992. The "Five Principles" were:

1. Respond promptly to all allegations of abuse;
2. Relieve the alleged offender promptly of his ministerial duties and refer him for
appropriate medical evaluation and intervention;
3. Comply with the obligations of civil law as regards reporting of the incident;
4. Reach out to the victims and their families;
5. Deal as openly as possible with the members of the community.[9]

(Much more of this is addressed in Chapters 11.)

Did the Church move as uniformly, swiftly, and forcefully as it could have? In retrospect, of course not. But one is hard-pressed to find another institution has done more work at cultivating a safe environment for children than the Catholic Church. Just in 2009 alone, the Church spent over $21 million in programs and procedures designed to protect children.[10]

The dwindling numbers of contemporaneous accusations affirm that the Church's measures have had a convincing impact in dramatically reducing incidents of abuse.

"The Catholic Church was at the forefront of this (addressing the problem of child abuse). I am not aware of any other organization that is doing as much as we're doing, and at such a cost," says Andy Eisenzimmer, chancellor for civil affairs for the Archdiocese of Saint Paul and Minneapolis.[11]

Martin Nussbaum is another individual with extensive experience with Catholic Church abuse cases. He is a veteran Colorado Springs attorney. "Almost all cases in litigation today involve allegations where the conduct occurred some time between 1960 and 1990," Nussbaum has told the Colorado Springs *Gazette*. "Since 2002, we have litigated cases where the conduct was alleged to have occurred in the 1930's, 1940's, 1950's, 1960's, 1970's, and 1980's. Very few thereafter. This is because the Catholic Church largely resolved the problem by 1992."[12]

The Church can now accurately affirm that it is protecting children in its care.

Dr. Monica Applewhite is a leading expert in studying organizations with histories of sexual abuse. She has worked with more than 300 organizations so that they can create safe environments that protect children. She has witnessed first-hand both the successes and failures of policies implemented by the Catholic Church. In March of 2009, the Irish Bishop's Conference invited her to Ireland for her assistance and expertise. Dr. Applewhite told her audience of bishops:

"We (in the United States) emerged from our crisis and began to move forward because of a decision that was made by our Catholic leaders. A decision to clarify the fundamental priority in matters of sexual abuse – from a focus on the life and value of the individual priest to a focus on the wellness of the Church as a Whole and the children of our Church as the primary representatives of this community."[13]

Yet would we know this from the media coverage?

Women "priests"?[14]

Hardly a day passes when someone is not opining that the Catholic Church ordain women as priests.

A May 2010 New York Times/CBS News poll reported that 59% of people who identified themselves as Catholic said they were in favor of women being ordained as priests.[15] Sadly, this demonstrates that a vast majority of Catholics simply do not know that this action is not a possibility.

Many people look at various Protestant denominations and their women clergy and wonder, "Why can't the Catholic Church do the same thing?"

Here's the key: Unlike in Protestant churches, the ordination of priests in the Catholic Church is a *sacrament*. The Catholic Church affirms that sacraments are gifts of God's grace. As Pope John Paul II wrote in his 1994 letter, *Ordinatio Sacerdotalis*, the Church simply *does not have the authority* to change the nature of something that Christ himself instituted.[16]

DOUBLE STANDARD

> The ordination of men as priests follows something that's far deeper than mere "tradition." It is a visible sign of God's grace. It is a gift. It must be respected and maintained.
>
> The priesthood is about *role*, not *power*. In his Letter to the Romans and his First Letter to the Corinthians, Paul teaches us about roles in the Church.[17] And the Catechism of the Catholic Church reminds us, "By creating the human being man and woman, God gives *personal dignity equally* to the one and the other" (emphasis added).[18]

NOTES AND REFERENCES

[1] George Weigel, "Church gets an unfair rap," *Philadelphia Inquirer*, April 4, 2010.

[2] Patrick J. Schiltz, "What the media missed in the sexual-abuse scandal," *Commonweal*, August 15, 2003.

[3] Ibid.

[4] Ibid.

[5] All four bulleted facts are from: John Jay College of Criminal Justice, "The Nature and Scope of the Problem of Sexual Abuse of Minors by Catholic Priests and Deacons in the United States," 2004. Available at http://www.usccb.org/nrb/

[6] Center for Applied Research in the Apostolate, "2009 Survey of Allegations and Costs: A Summary Report for the Secretariat of Child and Youth Protection, United States Conference of Catholic Bishops," Chapter Four, Georgetown University, Washington, D.C. February 2010.

[7] John Jay College of Criminal Justice, 2004.

[8] Tim Drake, "A Brief History of Abuse – And the Response To It," *National Catholic Register*, April 25-May 8, 2010 issue.

[9] Ibid.

[10] Ibid.

[11] Ibid.

[12] Mark Barna, "Springs attorney: Catholic sex abuse problem exaggerated," Colorado Springs *Gazette*, April 6th, 2010.

[13] "Address of Dr. Monica Applewhite to the Irish Bishops, March 10, 2009," The National Board for Safeguarding Children in the Catholic Church (Ireland), posted July 29, 2009, at http://www.safeguarding.ie/news-1/thevisitofdrmonicaapplewhite . Dr. Applewhite is the director of the consulting firm Confianza LLC in Austin, Texas.

[14] By no means is this an exhaustive explanation of why women cannot possibly be priests in the Catholic Church. In addition to Pope John Paul's 1994 letter (cited below), check out: "Women and the Priesthood" at Catholic Answers, http://www.catholic.com/library/Women_and_the_Priesthood.asp ... Joana Bogle, "Women Priests: No Chance," *This Rock*, October 1997 ... Alice Von Hildebrand and Peter Kreeft *Women and the Priesthood* (Steubenville, Ohio: Franciscan University Press, 1994).

[15] Laurie Goodstein and Dalia Sussman, "Catholics Criticize Pope on Abuse Scandal, but See Some Hope," *New York Times*, May 4, 2010 (see accompanying poll).

[16] Pope John Paul II, *Ordinatio Sacerdotalis*, Apostolic Letter, 22 May 1994. Available at http://www.vatican.va/holy_father/john_paul_ii/apost_letters/documents/hf_jp-ii_apl_22051994_ordinatio-sacerdotalis_en.html

[17] Romans 12:4-8; 1 Corinthians 12 (all)

[18] *Catechism of the Catholic Church*, paragraph 2393.

Two Sides

On July 16, 2007, Mark Gallegos and 507 other plaintiffs settled a $660 million lawsuit against the Archdiocese of Los Angeles, the largest payout by the Catholic Church in history.

Gallegos stood outside the Los Angeles County Courthouse facing an enormous gathering of cameramen and reporters. Standing with Gallegos were several plaintiff lawyers and many members of the advocacy group SNAP, the Survivors Network of Those Abused by Priests.

"I was raped by Father Sanchez when I was 8 years old. I was a good kid," Gallegos began. "[But] Father Sanchez took that away from me.

"I was a good kid. I wanted a good life for myself. I wanted a good life for my family. I come from a good family. And Father Sanchez took that away from me. I tried to commit suicide many times, many times over this."[1]

"Some people had relationships with their priest," Gallegos continued. "Not me. He raped me. That's what he did."[2]

Mr. Gallegos asserts that his life was never the same since the attack. As a teenager, he reportedly joined a notorious Pomona, California, street gang.[3] He also spent time in jail.[4]

"This isn't just about me," Gallegos announced. "This is about other people who've been victimized that can't come forward. It took me over 26 years to come forward and to talk about this."[5]

That night, hundreds of television newscasts across the country echoed Gallegos' words. International outlets also trumpeted Gallegos' story along with the news of the historic lawsuit.

The next day, every major morning news show and every major newspaper in the country prominently featured the historic settlement. The public heard of Gallegos' claims against Father Sanchez and of the despair which Gallegos claimed that he caused. Many papers carried a photo of Gallegos holding up his scarred wrists, which he claims he injured in his suicide attempt.

"[Father Sanchez] raped me in my gown. I ran out bleeding and ran to a (nearby) park crying," Gallegos once claimed.[6]

Yet in all of the massive coverage that transpired the day of the settlement and in the days after Gallegos' appearance, not a single journalist motioned to ask one obvious question: What did Father Sanchez have to say about all of this?

Father Sanchez is Father Manuel Sanchez Ontiveros. He was born in Spain, and he joined the priesthood there in 1954. In 1971, Father Sanchez came to the Unites States. In 1980, Father Sanchez became a pastor at Sacred Heart Parish in Pomona, California, the church at which Mr. Gallegos claims that the priest raped him in 1981.[7]

Two Sides

Responding to the awful charge against him, Father Sanchez has said he didn't even know his accuser. "I am completely innocent of the charges." The priest only learned of the claim against him in 2003, and he simply believed his accuser was either "looking for money or he sincerely confused me with another person."[8]

Gallegos' tale is "100 percent untrue," Sanchez has asserted. "With God as my witness, I am completely innocent of this claim of totally immoral and repugnant behavior. Being the object of a false accusation is a cause of great sorrow to me and my family."[9]

Yet in the frenzy of coverage of the historic lawsuit, not a single media outlet published Father Sanchez's denials. Neither did a single journalist ask any probing questions. For example, what did Gallegos mean when he once said, "He raped me in my gown"?

In over 46 years in ministry, no one except Mr. Gallegos accused Fr. Sanchez of any abuse or impropriety.

In 2003, the year of the accusation, utilizing former FBI agents and other investigators, the archdiocesan Clergy Misconduct Oversight Board studied the case and found "the evidence did not support the charges."[10] Again, not a single individual in the media reported this important fact during the coverage of the 2007 settlement.*

Another accuser to receive a sizable settlement the same day as Mr. Gallegos was an individual who had come forward in 2002 to allege that Fr. John P. Deady abused him between 1956 and 1957.

Born in 1913 and ordained in 1939, Fr. Deady served as a chaplain in the Navy during World War II. After that, his priesthood consisted of serving at a number of parishes in Southern California. Until 2002, no one had ever come forward to allege wrongdoing by the cleric. And as

DOUBLE STANDARD

with Fr. Sanchez, on the day of the settlement, no one from the media sought Fr. Deady's opinion of the charge against him. However, in this case, it was understandable.

Fr. Deady died eighteen years earlier, in 1989.[11]

In fact, in all of the coverage of the historic 2007 settlement, not a single media outlet reported that a full 30% of the priests who were accused in the Los Angeles Archdiocese were *deceased* at the time of their accusation.[12]

Declarations of innocence and dead priests. Would at least a brief mention of these factors have been the fair thing for the media to do for such a huge story? Did the media make an effort to provide context and fairness in this episode?

* I use the example of Mr. Gallegos and Rev. Sanchez as a typical example of a difficult case where both sides vehemently assert their claims. I do not mean to imply that anyone is lying, or one side is guilty or innocent. I *do* assert, however, that the media reported only *one* side of this particular case in their 2007 coverage.

NOTES AND REFERENCES

[1] Audio broadcast of the *The John & Ken Show*, KFI 640 AM, Los Angeles, July 16, 2007, 3pm hour.

[2] Tony Castro and Susan Abram, "The victims: For many, money won't erase scarring from abuse," *Daily News* (Los Angeles), July 17, 2007, p. 1.

Two Sides

[3] Jannise Johnson, "Man Alleges Priest Raped Him," *Daily Bulletin* (CA), March 27, 2006. Accessed from http://www.bishop-accountability.org/news2006/03_04/2006_03_27_Johnson_ManAlleges.htm

[4] Castro and Abram.

[5] Television news segment from *CBS 2 News*, Los Angeles, March 26, 2006.

[6] Johnson.

[7] Originally posted at the Archdiocese of Los Angeles web site, Msgr. Sanchez's history is available at http://www.nytimes.com/packages/pdf/national/20051012_PRIEST.pdf

[8] William Lobdell and Jean Guccione, "10 Priests in Lawsuits Still on Job," *Los Angeles Times*, February 7, 2004.

[9] *CBS 2 News*, Los Angeles, March 26, 2006.

[10] From the listing at http://bishop-accountability.org/priestdb/PriestDBbylastName-S.html

[11] Fr. Deady's history is available at http://www.nytimes.com/packages/pdf/national/20051012_PRIEST.pdf

[12] Information complied from "Archdiocese of Los Angeles: Accused," posted at http://www.bishop-accountability.org/usccb/natureandscope/dioceses/reports/losangelesca-rpt-list.pdf

7

The Voice of an Accused Priest

What about priests who refute the accusations against them?

Joe Maher is president and co-founder of Opus Bono Sacerdotii ("Work For the Good of the Priesthood").[1] Opus Bono Sacerdotii is a Detriot-based organization dedicated to assisting priests and religious who find themselves in crisis situations. According to Maher, over 5,000 priests in the United States alone have contacted his organization. Hundreds more from outside the U.S. have reached out to the group as well.

Opus Bono is able to provide emotional, spiritual, and logistical support to all priests, even those whose abuse is founded.

Mr. Maher and others at Opus Bono have witnessed first-hand the devastating effect that an abuse accusation has on a priest, especially if the priest vehemently asserts his innocence.

DOUBLE STANDARD

An accused priest sent the following letter to Mr. Maher at Opus Bono Sacerdotii in early 2010. It is truly sobering, as it provides an authentic perspective of a priest who experiences the public humiliation, feelings of hopelessness, and media whirlwind that accompany an abuse charge – in this case a charge that this priest forcefully denies.

Dear Mr. Maher,

I don't know where to begin. Those five words in the subject of this e-mail were some of the most difficult I ever had to write. A priest and friend gave me a flyer from Opus Bono two weeks ago and after I read of your ministry I felt I was given a direction or a glimpse of hope that someone might understand. And so, with all humility I extend my arm and hand to you.

Until a priest has to personally experience the pain and degradation of being removed from priestly service, there is no one who can possibly 'understand.' This year, I will observe (I cannot say celebrate) my 40th anniversary of ordination as a Roman Catholic priest. This past June, I had a surprise visit to my parish office by two officials from the chancery, the vicar for priests and a canon lawyer (who happens to be a classmate of mine). They asked to see me privately and I was extremely nervous because of their attitude and demeanor. When the three of us were alone, they proceeded to tell me that a 'credible allegation of sexual abuse' was made against me and that I had an hour to pack a bag and to come with them. Few details were given to me when I asked.

They mentioned a name which I never heard of before and that this 'victim' was deceased. His widow and attorney came to the diocese to bring this supposed abuse

The Voice of an Accused Priest

to their attention. This was to have occurred some thirty years ago. I have served in my parish as pastor for almost 20 years without the slightest hint of any impropriety.

As I left with them in utter disbelief, shame and humiliation, I discovered later that the diocese had already sent out a 'Fax Blast' concerning my removal. After the press and media extensively exposed my 'credible allegation of sexual abuse' for two days, I found myself living in a hellish nightmare. After some two or three weeks later, the same two officials called me to another meeting and informed me that another 'victim' came forth after the public disclosure to make a second allegation against me. (And I had thought that life could not have possibly gotten any worse.)

As God as my witness, I swear as I swore on a Bible before the diocesan officials, these allegations are totally and completely untrue. My mind and my soul are bruised, beaten and trampled down. My parishioners are most supportive but I am not permitted to visit them and I cannot afford to call them by telephone. My health is not good and I had avoided many appointments with my doctors. This past Christmas Eve and Christmas Day were the worst emotionally devastating events I have ever had to endure. I was close to suicide. I suffer panic attacks, acute anxiety and severe depression. Worst of all, there is nobody that can really understand or share this onerous burden that I bear.

I am in financial ruin 'to put the icing on the cake.' I have exhausted my life savings trying to pay monthly expenses for car lease payments, auto insurance, telephone, and many credit card companies to mention a few.

DOUBLE STANDARD

Even when the day for my exoneration and restoration does come, I have already seen the future. There is none. Two weeks ago a fellow priest of our diocese was accused of sexual misconduct which allegedly occurred forty years prior, was exonerated and was officially assigned to serve 'in restricted ministry' at a convent motherhouse. When the media got hold of his new assignment, the public outcry that a 'priest, accused of credible sexual abuse' would be assigned to an area which had schools and day-care centers nearby, our bishop, bowing to 'public pressure and shepherdly concern' reversed and revoked his official assignment the very next day, not even twenty-four hours had elapsed.

Now I have abandoned all hope. I do not know where to turn for help, for someone who understands. I am ashamed. I am alone. I reach out for your hand.

'Father John'[2]

Mr. Maher reports that letters such as these are "typical."[3] Once a mob of media outlets grabs a hold of an accusation, the public presumption of guilt is firmly planted. Meanwhile, the priest is essentially alone and defenseless.

"As a Chicago lawyer that defends priests told me," Maher relays, "'Priests are guilty until proven guiltier.'"[4]

Other defense attorneys agree. "How does the process react in the face of huge publicity? Not well, I'm afraid," says Timothy P. O'Neill, Jr. "The full story needs still to be written. At this point, priests have no voice."[5]

When will the media change its unfair approach? When will it give a voice to those like "Father John"?

The Voice of an Accused Priest

A caution about local newscasts and radio hosts

While looking at the anti-Catholic slant of major newspapers like the *Boston Globe* and the *New York Times*, it's easy to overlook the similar tendencies of local television newscasts and radio shows. And as is the case with newspapers, these outlets often lose a sense of perspective when trumpeting a story.

For example, in June 2010, the Archdiocese of Boston released a statement that it would be putting a parish priest on leave because someone came forward to accuse the priest of abuse *50 years earlier*. The priest had no history of accusations and was now 82 years old. The *Boston Globe* leaped on the story, and then local television stations got in on the action.

Although there were almost no details about the case to report (*e.g.*, the nature of the abuse, the age of the victim at the time of the abuse, where it took place, etc.), every local television station in Boston featured the story prominently in their newscasts. One station even breathlessly sent a reporter on the scene to the priest's church "with the latest," although there was absolutely nothing to report beyond the contents of the short statement that the archdiocese had already released. From the urgency that the newscasts presented, one would have thought the allegation was of recent abuse, not of five decades ago.

Meanwhile, the priest is on leave pending an investigation. What if the investigation finds no evidence to support the charges? What if exculpatory evidence clears the priest? Will these same newscasts leap on the story "with the latest"? Stay tuned.

Across the country in Los Angeles, the top-rated afternoon radio show is the *John & Ken Show* on KFI 640 AM. The hosts' disdain for the Catholic Church cannot be overstated. Every few months, the hosts insist on revisiting the *same* case of abuse in the Los Angeles archdiocese, dating from 1986. Indeed, the case of former priest Michael Baker is the "one that troubles me the most," according to Cardinal Roger Mahony. The Cardinal has apologized on numerous occasions for not fully removing Baker from ministry and calling the police when he learned in 1986 that Baker abused boys. Despite the efforts by the archdiocese to monitor him, Baker continued to abuse until he was laicized in 2000. Hosts John Kobylt and Ken Chiampou continue to rail against the Cardinal for his biggest decades-old mistake. On a June 2010 broadcast, the hosts welcomed California victims' attorney John C. Manly, whom they regularly invite to berate the Cardinal over the same Baker case. In a span of just minutes, Manly and the hosts pounded the Cardinal as a "consummate power whore," a "sociopath," a "psychopath," a "Mafia boss," and a "dark, dark, foul person." Kobylt formulated that "kids were raped for [Cardinal Mahony's] own ambition" ("to be the Pope," apparently) and that Mahony "doesn't have a conscience." Kobylt then postulated that the Cardinal likely "has pedophile tendencies" and "likes to rape boys himself."[6]

Does the Cardinal merit criticism for his handling of the Baker case? Sure. But any clear-thinking listener can see that John and Ken's presentation is a bit over the top considering the number of years that have passed. Mean-

The Voice of an Accused Priest

> while, these hosts have not been nearly as vitriolic over the far-more-recent cases of abuse and cover-ups happening right under their noses in the Los Angeles Unified School District (see Chapters 3 and 4).

NOTES AND REFERENCES

[1] Opus Bono Sacerdotii ("Work For the Good of the Priesthood"), 3430 East Jefferson Avenue, Suite 309, Detroit, Michigan 48207. Phone: (313) 937-6305. The web site is www.opusbono.org

[2] Telephone interview with Joe Maher, Tuesday, July 13, 2010.

[3] Letter printed with kind permission from Joe Maher, Opus Bono.

[4] Telephone interview with Joe Maher.

[5] Kevin Cullen, "Phony cases a danger in abuse battle: Investigators use care, but can't always be sure," *Boston Globe*, August 5, 2002, p. A1.

[6] The *John & Ken Show*, KFI 640 AM, Los Angeles, June 15, 2010, 2pm hour.

"Repressed Memories"?

One seriously underreported element of the narrative that is the Catholic Church abuse scandals is that many alleged victims have surfaced with their charges after claiming they "repressed" memories of their abuse for periods of years, often decades, and then "recovered" them.

As always, we must be mindful and sensitive in dealing with this subject. Of course, not all victims of clergy abuse claim "recovered memory." The pain of sexual abuse is all too devastatingly real. Prayers, compassion, and justice must always be pursued for abuse victims.

What are the theories of "repressed memory" and "recovered memory"? According to proponents of the theories, while millions of adults have lived their entire lives with the awful memories of real abuse they suffered, individuals with so-called "repressed memory" have no actual recall of abuse. Proponents claim that the terrorizing and traumatizing nature of abuse causes the victim to "repress," or essentially forget, the memory of the actual abuse happening. Later on in their lives, when these individuals encounter depression, unsuccessful pursuits, or other problems in their lives, therapists convince them that all of their problems stem from childhood abuse that they have "repressed." Using suggestive questioning and other techniques, the therapists then cajole their subjects into "recovering" "memories" of childhood sex abuse.

This appears to be the case with a New Hampshire woman, age 44. In March of 2010, she came forward to publicly announce that her parish priest had kissed and fondled her for over a year and a half starting in 1979 when she was 13. The small-town *Eagle-Tribune* newspaper of North Andover, Massachusetts, reported the woman's story. For starters, the woman said she had no memory of any abuse by the priest for over 30 years. In fact, the priest she accused actually married her and her first husband. But she claims that after two divorces and battles with eating disorders, "Everything started flooding back in all at once." How did this happen? The woman said she had a "dream" and then discussed it with her therapist. "With the help of her therapist, [the woman] gradually began uncovering her past ... and the abuse and pain she had been hiding from," wrote the *Eagle-Tribune*.[1] Yet the newspaper's profile never defined what the woman's therapist appears to have practiced: recovered-memory therapy.

Rather, the paper added that she was "awaiting a decision on a claim with the Archdiocese that could award her upwards of $75,000."[2] Working to the woman's advantage was the fact that the priest she accused was a laicized abuser whose record of harm was already established.

A month later, the *Boston Globe* featured the same woman in an Associated Press article about how alleged abuse victims were reacting to the recent "crisis" involving decades-old allegations of clergy abuse in Europe. The paper relayed the woman's sad tale of abuse, but it made no mention at all of her therapist or that that recovered-

"Repressed Memories"?

memory therapy may have played a role in her claim. The AP presented the woman's claims as simple matters of fact.[3]

What almost all journalists have failed to report, however, is that there is no scientific evidence that "recovered memory" is genuine at all. In fact, many experts in the field of psychology and memory science have flat-out discredited the theory.

"Recovered-memory therapy will come to be recognized as the quackery of the 20th century," Richard Ofshe, a social psychologist at the University of California, Berkeley, has said.[4]

"If penis envy made us look dumb, this will make us look totally gullible," adds Paul McHugh, chairman of the psychiatry department at Johns Hopkins University.[5]

The truth is that people who have remembered their childhood abuse their whole lives have a clearer and more detailed memory of being abused. They also report more intense feelings.[6] This science is in line with studies involving Holocaust survivors and war veterans. These studies have consistently found that "the difficulty for those people is not remembering their ordeals, but forgetting them."[7]

After a six-year study, Harvard psychology professor Richard J. McNally wrote a book about memory and child abuse called *Remembering Trauma*.[8] "The notion that the mind protects itself by banishing the most disturbing, terrifying events is psychiatric folklore," McNally has said. "The more traumatic and stressful something is, the less likely someone is to forget it."[9]

Yet because of the partnerships between journalists, victim lawyers, and advocacy groups, the debunked theory of "repressed memory" remains almost universally unchallenged in our nation's media.

DOUBLE STANDARD

Elizabeth Loftus, professor of psychology at the University of California Irvine, has been dubbed "the most influential female psychologist of the past century," and she may be the world's leading researcher on memory.[10] Her years of work debunking the theory of repressed memory has made her not only an authority, but her work has enabled individuals falsely accused of awful sex crimes to be exonerated.

Dr. Loftus has numerous studies to her credit that show that memories can be distorted. She has also demonstrated that totally false memories can be planted in people's minds. For example, in experiments Dr. Loftus has been able to plant the false memories of "getting lost for an extended time as a child, facing a threat to one's life as a child, witnessing demonic possession as a child, seeing wounded animals as part of a traumatic bombing, and more."[11] Loftus' book, authored with Katherine Ketchum, *The Myth of Repressed Memory*,[12] is very well known and respected in the psychology field.

"Memory can be changed, inextricably altered, and that what we think we know, what we believe with all our hearts, is not necessarily the truth," says Dr. Loftus.[13] As for the claim that people are able to "repress" traumatic events, she says, "You can't be raped for 10 years and not remember it. Yet, according to the repression aficionados, anything's possible."[14]

Back in 1993, the media widely reported the story of a young man who accused Chicago Cardinal Joseph Bernardin of abuse. It was a prominent story for several days.

But then the accuser of Cardinal Bernardin, who had done several high-profile interviews, including an emotional and tearful "recollection" on CNN, essentially recanted his story. He acknowledged that his claims were

"Repressed Memories"?

based on "recovered memory" that had surfaced through hypnosis. He dropped his $10 million lawsuit against Bernardin and another priest, admitting that his memory was "not reliable."

Yet nearly two decades later, the media continues far too often to profile an alleged victim without mentioning that recovered memory therapy may have played a role in "remembering" the alleged "abuse." (Another example would be the case involving California Bishop Tod David Brown. When the *Los Angeles Times* reported that a man had claimed Brown abused him as a boy decades earlier, the paper made no mention at all of the fact that the man only "remembered" the alleged abuse after a therapist appeared to have practiced recovered-memory therapy on him.)

Why are so many people who go to therapy willing to accept such a wild theory of "repressed memory"?

Dr. Loftus explains, "In many cases, you have an excuse for all your problems. If you've misbehaved or haven't achieved as much as you should have, or you're depressed or have other symptoms, now you have an explanation. You're not a bad person, you're not a crazy person, you're just abused. You get bathed in a love bath by other supposed victims and victim supporters, you get sympathy and empathy — there's the benefit."[15]

It's seldom that writers at major newspapers confront the issue of repressed memory. This is likely because columnists don't want to give off the impression that they're alienating abuse victims. And journalists certainly don't want to offend these alleged victims' lawyers, who are very often the sources of their stories to begin with. Columnists are always on the lookout for good stories, and profiles of crime victims, especially if the alleged perpetrator is a Catholic priest, are always of high human interest. If a lawyer feeds a good story to a columnist, there is certainly no incentive for the writer to challenge the veracity of it. And while such a practice certainly works very well for the alleged victim's lawyer and the client, the public is ill-served and sometimes misled.

In the rare moments that journalists have addressed the role of recovered-memory therapy in some clergy abuse cases, writers have been less-than-honest in addressing the issue. For example, in a 2003 column in the *Boston Globe*, columnist Eileen McNamara was addressing a Boston clergy case in which recovered-memory therapy played a role. McNamara snipped, "It defies belief, but not possibility, that the Catholic Church in Boston intends to suggest in court that this scandal is nothing but a figment of the victims' imagination."[16] The Church never claimed, of course, that the *entire scandal* was "nothing but a figment of the victims' imagination," but in this particular case, it felt that the accuser's claim was untrue.

When there is no science to support recovered-memory therapy, McNamara exemplifies the sort of rhetoric that some journalists have resorted to.

Again, this is a component of the clergy abuse narrative that must be approached with caution and sensitivity. However, journalists have the responsibility in disclosing to their readers if an abuse claim arose from dubious therapy techniques. It is only fair to the accused individual. It is incredibly traumatic for any person, not just a Catholic priest, to face a public accusation of child abuse. Nowadays, there is far too often the presumption of "guilty until proven innocent," and journalists have certainly contributed to this sentiment being so common.

"Repressed Memories"?

NOTES AND REFERENCES

[1] Brian Messenger, "Time to heal: After 30 years, local woman speaks about clergy abuse," *Eagle-Tribune* (North Andover, MA), March 28, 2010.

[2] Ibid.

[3] Jay Lindsay, "For US abuse victims, crisis reawakens past trauma," *Boston Globe*, April 8, 2010.

[4] Leon Jaroff and Jeanne McDowell, "Repressed-Memory Therapy: Lies of the Mind," *Time*, November 29, 1993.

[5] Ibid.

[6] Loftus, E.F., Polonsky, S., & Fullilove, M. T. (1994). Memories of childhood sexual abuse: Remembering and repressing. *Psychology of Women Quarterly*, 18, 67-845.

[7] Benjamin Radford, "Validity of 'Repressed Memories' Challenged in Court," *LiveScience*, September 15, 2009. Downloaded from http://www.livescience.com/strangenews/090915-repressed-memories.html

[8] Richard J. McNally, *Remembering Trauma* (Cambridge, Mass.: Belknap Press of Harvard University Press, 2005).

[9] Daniel Lyons, "Sex, God & Greed," *Forbes*, June 9, 2003.

[10] Amy Wilson, "War & remembrance," *Orange County Register*, November 3, 2002.

[11] "Elizabeth F. Loftus: Award for Distinguished Scientific Applications of Psychology," *American Psychologist*, Vol. 58, No. 11, 2003, p. 865.

[12] Elizabeth Loftus and Katherine Ketchum, *The Myth of Repressed Memories* (New York: St. Martin's Griffin, 1994).

[13] Elizabeth Loftus, "Dear Mother: Facing the Loss of a Parent: The personal story of losing a parent," *Psychology Today*, May 1, 2003.

[14] Sasha Abramsky, "Memory and Manipulation: The trials of Elizabeth Loftus, defender of the wrongly accused," *LA Weekly*, August 19, 2004.

[15] Karl Sabbagh, "Seeking the truth about false memory," *London Times*, January 8, 2004.

[16] Eileen McNamara, "Still Catholic, but changed," *Boston Globe*, March 9, 2003.

SNAP and Friends

Most certainly, Catholics are obligated to genuinely demonstrate the utmost compassion and sympathy for those individuals who were harmed by priests.

Unfortunately, a small number of those who have been abused by Catholic clergy have not always engaged the public honestly when discussing the Church and the scandals.

The leading voice speaking for the victims of Catholic clergy abuse is the group SNAP, the Survivors Network of Those Abused by Priests. For nearly two decades, whether it is television, newspaper, or radio, the media has regularly granted SNAP an open and welcome platform for railing against the Catholic Church for its handling of the abuse scandal.

Indeed, SNAP has been correct that priests terribly violated innocent youths and many bishops failed to properly take action when notified of suspected abuse. The group has also been helpful to those victims who may have felt alone in their injuries.

SNAP's public presentation, however, is another issue. Their public pronouncements are often rife with unfair hyperbole, and their statements can be false and misleading. Meanwhile, their harmonious relationship with aggressive lawyers raises serious questions about the group's true motives.

SNAP claims that its organization's "primary purpose is to provide support for men and women who have been sexually victimized by members of the clergy."[1] However, SNAP's own tax filings reveal that the organization does very little in terms of concrete "support." In 2007, when the organization posted revenue of over $470,000, SNAP's own records show that they listed only a paltry $593 being spent for "Survivor Support."[2] Many other years, there is no entry for "Survivor Support" at all.[3] Not surprisingly, according to the Reliability Report for SNAP by the Better Business Bureau (BBB), SNAP "does not meet one or more of the [BBB's] 20 standards for Charity Accountability."[4]

A common complaint about the Catholic Church from spokespeople of SNAP is the Church's supposed "lack of transparency." Yet SNAP demonstrates very little transparency of its own. SNAP absolutely refuses to divulge the names of contributors to the organization. They claim that this is to protect the "privacy of victims."[5] (As if only a victim could contribute to the group?)

Obtaining information about SNAP's donors is frustratingly difficult. Yet evidence indicates that significant supporters of SNAP are lawyers who represent alleged victims of abuse. In September of 2003, *Forbes* magazine's Daniel Lyons was able to report that SNAP's largest contributor in 2002 was Laurence Drivon, a leading victim attorney. The theatrical Jeff Anderson donated $10,000 in 2002 and then offered up to $50,000 in 2003.[6]

In the last several years, SNAP has been successful in keeping a lid on the names of lawyers who give to the organization.

But the question remains: Is there an informal *quid pro quo* between SNAP and lawyers in which contributions by lawyers is returned in the form of referrals? SNAP, along with lawyers, vehemently deny this, but it sure seems like it. St. Louis attorney Ken Chackes openly admitted in 2010 that his firm contributed money to SNAP, and SNAP funneled potential business to his office by giving accusers his phone number.[7] The arrangement is not explicit or in writing, of course. "We don't have any sort of arrangement with SNAP," said Chackes. He only acknowledged that his firm donated money to the group "like we would to any not-for-profit organization."[8] Yet one cannot help but wonder from what other "not-for-profit" organizations Chackes would benefit so handsomely from.

Meanwhile, the intimate relationship between SNAP and lawyers cannot be denied, as they often appear to work cooperatively. Jeff Anderson of Minnesota regularly makes SNAP a visible component of his dramatic press conferences.

So what does SNAP actually *do*? Judging from their tax returns, the organization provides little in terms of concrete support. In addition to publicly lambasting the Church, it seems a primary function is to direct business to lawyers. With over $2 billion in settlements against the Church in the United States alone, SNAP has been quite successful.

The Catholic clergy scandals have also proved quite profitable for the leaders of SNAP. From 2004 to 2008, the organization received nearly $3.3 million in contributions.[9] In 2008, founder Barbara Blaine and national director David Clohessy each took home $75,750.[10] (In Missouri, where Clohessy resides, that would more than double the starting salary of a school teacher with a master's degree.[11])

Meanwhile, not all victims of clergy sex abuse are supporters of SNAP. A number of victims have been unhappy with what they see as secrecy, hypocrisy, and duplicity in the organization.

> "I'm a victim too and these groups provide witness expertise and then get major payoffs. It's a racket. I dropped out of the 2004 Pittsburgh case because they weren't addressing abuse by nuns, only priests. Silent victims get nothing but you can be sure that the lawyers and groups get their money."[12]

There have also been complaints that SNAP has threatened legal action and banned victims at the SNAP Internet discussion board for merely criticizing the organization.[13]

SNAP also enjoys a very friendly relationship with the media. The *Dallas Blog* reported that Barbara Blaine, SNAP's president, has "established a 'network' of reporters in 'all corners of the country' who closely work with SNAP."[14]

In March of 2010, days before the *New York Times* splashed its flimsy tale trying to connect Pope Benedict to a decades-old case of clergy abuse, SNAP sent out a mass e-mail asking victims to contact a "New York reporter" to tell their stories.[15] In other words, SNAP's relationship with the media appears to be so cozy that they were privy to the fact that the *Times* was working on a high-profile story about Catholic Church abuse.

How did SNAP learn this? The most likely informer is attorney Jeff Anderson, who provided background documents to the *Times*.

SNAP and Friends

By the way, when the *Times* later published its big, front-page piece, members of SNAP just-so-happened to be protesting at the Vatican. The feature provided a nice extra visual component for the media to report.

NOTES AND REFERENCES

1   SNAP's 2007 IRS Form 990 filing. Downloaded in May of 2010 from http://www.illinoisattorneygeneral.gov/charities/search/index.jsp

2   Ibid.

3   Review of SNAP's IRS Form 990 filings in May 2010.

4   The statement is found at the site of the Better Business Bureau (BBB), June 2010, http://www.bbb.org/stlouis/business-reviews/charity-soliciting-locally/survivors-network-for-those-abused-by-priests-in-saint-louis-mo-310345838 . SNAP posts that it is screened and endorsed by an organization called "Independent Charities of America" (ICA). However, this author could find nothing on ICA's web which allowed visitors to complain to the ICA about any of their charities. (This possibility is clearly visible at the BBB.) ICA's "Eligibility Standards" seemed awfully weak, in this author's opinion, as it appeared to consist largely of just having all of your federal paperwork in proper order and your fundraising materials being "truthful and nondeceptive."

5   Tim Townsend, "Advocate for those abused by priest ramps up since European scandal," St. Louis *Post-Dispatch*, April 18, 2010.

6   Daniel Lyons, "Paid to Picket," *Forbes*, September 15, 2003.

7   Ibid.

8   Townsend.

9   IRS Form 990 review conducted in May 2010 using forms posted from http://www.illinoisattorneygeneral.gov/charities/search/index.jsp

[10] Townsend.

[11] "Missouri," http://www.teachingtips.com/average-teacher-salaries/missouri/. Downloaded May 2010.

[12] Letter read aloud and shown on "Riz Khan – Pope Benedict's Challenge," Al Jazeera English, Season 2010 Ep. 54, April 14, 2010. Interview with the Catholic League's William Donohue and SNAP's David Clohessy. Viewed at http://www.youtube.com/watch?v=44ZHCP6PflE

[13] "Misplaced Anger," posted at http://unsnap.blogspot.com/2007/02/misplaced-anger.html. Downloaded May 2010. This site appears to have been created by a Southern California abuse victim.

[14] Tom McGregor, "Guardian UK Defends Pope Benedict XVI," *Dallas Blog*, April 17, 2010. http://www.dallasblog.com/201004171006395/dallas-blog/guardian-uk-defends-pope-benedict-xvi.html

[15] Tom McGregor, "Jeff Anderson Uses SNAP to Recruit Sex Abuse Clients," *Dallas Blog*, April 6, 2010. http://www.dallasblog.com/201004061006346/dallas-blog/jeff-anderson-uses-snap-to-recruit-sex-abuse-clients.html

10

An ACORN in SNAP

The most visible presence of SNAP may be its high-profile national director, David Clohessy. He has appeared on scores of television programs over the past two decades. Popular forums such as *Oprah* and *60 Minutes* have featured him.

Raised in Missouri, David Clohessy claims he was molested by a priest when he was between the ages of about 12 and 16 (about 1969 to 1973). Clohessy then says he "repressed"[1] memories of the abuse until he was about 32 years old, claiming a viewing of the 1988 movie *Nuts*, featuring Barbra Streisand as a child abuse victim, led him to "remember" the abuse.[2] Clohessy filed suit against the Jefferson City diocese in which the priest worked, but the case was dismissed because 18 years had passed and the statute of limitations had expired. After being removed from ministry by the diocese in 1992, the accused man reportedly resigned from the priesthood, and it has been reported that he now works as a flight attendant.[3]

When railing against the Church, many of Clohessy's public statements have centered on a common theme:

Church officials failed to protect children when they did not call the police when suspected or actual abuse was reported to them. Clohessy has frequently called on the Church and the public to "break the silence" and report abuse and "cover-ups." Among his pronouncements:

>- "When any citizen suspects a crime, he or she should call the police"[4]
>- "Actions protect kids, not words"[5]
>- "You've got to err on the side of protecting the physical and emotional safety of children rather than the reputation of one adult."[6]

Yet there is a very notable, yet little-known, episode in Clohessy's own life in which, when confronted with the opportunity to report suspected child abuse, he failed to do so.

David Clohessy happens to be the brother of a Catholic priest, Kevin Clohessy, and Kevin has been accused of child sexual abuse. In 1991, Kevin was accused of molesting a male college student. Two years later, the diocese substantiated the claim, silently removed him from ministry, and quietly sent him to treatment. In 1995, the diocese surreptitiously reassigned Kevin to a parish. Then, in 2000, Kevin unexpectedly requested a leave of absence. Three years later, a man came forward to allege that Clohessy had continuously abused him as a minor between 1984 and 1993.[7]

Quite astonishingly, there is evidence that David Clohessy, *while he was a spokesman for SNAP*, had the opportunity to report suspected child abuse to the police, but he did not do so. According to a 2002 profile in the *St. Louis Post-Dispatch*, "in the mid-1990s, people [had]

An ACORN in SNAP

started telling [David] that his brother was sexually molesting other young men ... Clohessy didn't tell police."[8]

Meanwhile, another 2002 profile reported the similar story:

> David said he had known for years about the allegations and agonized over whether to report his brother to authorities. He even contemplated distributing leaflets outside his brother's church. But in the end, he did not go to the police.
> "It will probably be a quandary until the day I die," said David.[9]

Again, Clohessy was already a public advocate speaking out against abuse in the Church and the inaction of Church officials in their handling of abuse cases. Yet when the opportunity came for David himself to blow the whistle and remove a possible child molester from ministry and away from kids, he failed to do so.

"He told me he was getting help, getting treatment," David said of his brother.[10]

Again, on a number of occasions, Clohessy and the folks at SNAP have lambasted the Church for its past belief that treatment was adequate enough for an abuser. Indeed, it was the faulty belief in the psychological community up until the early 1980's that pedophiles could be "cured" of their condition with proper treatment. (See Chapter 12.) Nowadays we know how terribly erroneous and harmful that belief is.

Yet Clohessy has implied that treatment seemed to be an appropriate measure for his brother.

Here is a clear-cut example of a double standard. Yet you'd be hard-pressed to find someone in the media questioning David Clohessy about this episode. He has incessantly called for others to come forward to report suspected child abuse when he himself stood quiet and covered for his abusive brother.

Although Mr. Clohessy's response with regards to his brother appears to be a clear case of hypocrisy, it is only right to address the episode with sensitivity and empathy. Clohessy himself has articulated that the entire chapter has been an excruciating trial for him and his entire family.[11]

A frustration lies, however, with Clohessy not appearing to apply his own personal experience with his brother to the experience of the Catholic Church.

Surely there's a parallel between Clohessy's inaction with the inaction of Church officials in not reporting abuse.

No one wants to believe that someone so close in their life could have acted so wrongly. It's only natural.

A tidal wave of feelings must have been running through David's head as he tried to grapple with the fact that his brother had harmed children. It is something everyone should be mindful and considerate of.

Yet surely these same feelings were experienced by Church officials during the 1970's and 1980's when they were notified about abusive priests. The Church surely felt, given the pastoral and caring nature of the institution rooted in the teachings of Jesus Christ, that it was well equipped to address the problem of abusive priests and "rectify" the situation. Church officials must have said to themselves, "Isn't *healing* a central component of the Church's mission?"

Such a thinking helps *explain* – but not *excuse* – why bishops and others acted the way they did. It is frustrating that Clohessy has not seemed to acknowledge this.

An ACORN in SNAP

Today, now we know better. Unless an offender is completely segregated from children, there is an all-too-high risk that the individual may offend again. Meanwhile, kids are terribly injured and are not given the help and support that they so desperately need.

Since the mid-1980's, the Church has made huge strides in making itself an organization that is a safe environment for children. (See Chapters 5 and 11.) No other institution even comes close to undergoing the transformations that the Church has.

But Clohessy and SNAP have been steadfast in not acknowledging these efforts. Often they just dismiss them. They continue on their relentless attack no matter what the Church does. Why?

Clohessy's professional background may explain this approach.

Before his career with SNAP, Mr. Clohessy was heavily involved in the notorious community organization ACORN (Association of Community Organizations for Reform Now). He spent almost a decade with a Missouri chapter of the controversial group.

ACORN is a sprawling political grassroots organization that has committed itself since 1970 to pursuing "social and economic justice" across the United States. Under the declaration of helping low-income neighborhoods and low-income workers, its activities often target individuals from large corporations and government entities. The group is notorious for applying aggressive, in-your-face tactics and relentless attacks against its opponents. A not-so-untypical action by ACORN is one that took place in Baltimore in the late 1990's. In protesting the position of the city's mayor, ACORN sent four busloads of protesters to his house, where members screamed obscenities at the mayor's wife and family.[12] In addition, "[a]s recently as June 2009, an angry mob of at least 150 ACORN protesters nearly knocked New York state Sen. James Alesi, a Republican, down to the floor and also spat in the face of his chief of staff."[13]

The roots of these strong-arm strategies come from a well-known figure named Saul Alinsky, a radical community organizer from the 1950's to his death in 1972. Alinsky authored an influential book called *Rules for Radicals*.[14] Community organizers have long considered it the handbook of strategies to guide their anti-corporate and economic pursuits.

According to Alinsky's *Rules*, it is the duty of community organizers to agitate people into action. An effective organizer relentlessly and unapologetically demonizes his opponent. The use of ridicule is also essential (Rule #5), and it's imperative that organizers never let up the pressure on their opponent (Rule #8). These fundamentals are applied to ultimately extort the target. It's only fitting that Alinsky acknowledges Satan in the dedication pages of his book. ("Lest we not forget at least an over-the-shoulder acknowledgement to the very first radical … the very first radical who rebelled against the establishment and did that he at least won his own kingdom – Lucifer."[15])

One of Clohessy's most notable episodes as a leader with ACORN was in 1991. At the time Clohessy was with the group, it was common for ACORN workers to stand at busy St. Louis stoplights and harass drivers to promote their causes. As ACORN workers dangerously weaved between cars handing out fliers, they made traffic even worse. Traffic lights would turn green, yet ACORN workers would still be weaving through lanes hustling for their group. St. Louis County eventually cited ACORN for breaking the law disallowing solicitation on St. Louis

An ACORN in SNAP

roadways. After the citation, Clohessy and ACORN sued the county, claiming their first-amendment rights were being violated. ACORN and Clohessy lost the case, as the United States Eighth Circuit Court of Appeals upheld the citation by St. Louis County.[16]

As we'll see in subsequent pages, ruthless aggressiveness is a key trait of SNAP; and this characteristic, orchestrated largely by Clohessy, has the fingerprints of Alinsky and ACORN all over it.

It's apparent that Clohessy has faithfully applied his experience in ACORN and the tactics of Alinsky to his position of national spokesperson for SNAP, and these influences are emblematic of how SNAP operates as an organization.

Alinsky's approach works well for SNAP, because there are few topics that enrage more than the sexual abuse of a child. Clohessy and SNAP are able to take advantage of this sentiment very well. For fear of "insulting the victims" of abuse, journalists will rarely, if ever, challenge their claims, no matter how wild.

SNAP will respond to even the slightest defense of the Catholic Church with a vicious and pointed response. If one dares to question the validity of a decades-old allegation of abuse against a dead priest surfaced through the discredited practice of "recovered-memory therapy," SNAP will surely attack such a questioner for "rubbing salt on the wounds of victims" and "defending child abuse."

Here is a typical example of how SNAP attacks Church officials:

On Palm Sunday 2010, Archbishop Timothy Dolan of New York addressed the false attacks on the Pope in the media that had occurred during Lent. In discussing the issue, Dolan readily acknowledged, "Anytime this horror, vicious sin, and nauseating crime is reported, as it needs to be, victims and their families are wounded again." He then asked his audience, "Does the Church and her Pastor, Pope Benedict XVI, need intense scrutiny and just criticism for tragic horrors long past?"

"Yes! Yes!" Dolan answered. "[The Pope] himself has asked for it, encouraging complete honesty."

Archbishop Dolan simply begged, "All we ask is that it be fair and that the Catholic Church not be singled out for a horror that has cursed every culture, religion, organization, institution, school, agency and family in the world."[17]

What was SNAP's response to Dolan's remarks? In a nasty press statement the next day, SNAP accused Dolan of showing "callousness and narrowness that ill-befits the head of a religious institution." Then they said Dolan's words "attacked abuse victims." And if that weren't enough, SNAP also charged Dolan with "fostering a climate" that "demeans [and] attacks child-sex victims."[18]

One can see that charity is not part of SNAP's repertoire.

In his *Rules for Radicals*, Saul Alinsky wrote, "Pick the target, freeze it, personalize it, and polarize it … [I]solate the target from sympathy. Go after people and not institutions; people hurt faster than institutions. (This is cruel, but very effective. Direct, personalized criticism and ridicule works.)" (This is Rule #12.)[19]

The Dolan episode is a textbook example of SNAP applying an Alinsky tactic. The fact that SNAP's attack was dishonest and false did not matter to the group. SNAP is determined to "pick the target," "isolate the target from sympathy," and personally hurt it.

SNAP: Pro-lawsuit or anti-lawsuit?

If a priest claims that he is falsely accused, should that priest sue his accuser?

If you go to SNAP for an answer, you might get two different responses.

In 2006, when a Chicago-area priest countersued his accuser, Barbara Blaine, the president of SNAP, charged that the maneuver was "a hardball legal tactic that is unbecoming of an alleged spiritual figure." She complained that the priest was "simply trying to intimidate other witnesses and victims."[20]

Two years later, in 2008, Blaine co-authored a letter to former New York City mayor Rudolph Giuliani, who was seeking the Republican Presidential nomination. Monsignor Alan Placa, a longtime friend and employee of Giuliani, was accused of child sex abuse but officials never filed criminal charges. Placa vehemently maintained his innocence. Complaining of the association between the candidate and Placa, Blaine sniped at Giuliani in the letter, "Both you and Msgr. Placa have had five years to take legal action against all those who have allegedly 'falsely accused' Placa."[21]

"Take legal action"? One can only assume that if the monsignor *did* file charges, SNAP would then grumble that it was "unbecoming of an alleged spiritual figure."

Same organization. Two different attacks.

DOUBLE STANDARD

NOTES AND REFERENCES

[1] David Clohessy, "In the Trenches," *Journal of Religion & Abuse*, Vol. 6(2) 2004, 31-39.

[2] Frank Bruni, "Am I My Brother's Keeper?" *New York Times Magazine*, May 12, 2002.

[3] "Database of Publicly Accused Priests in the United States," http://www.bishop-accountability.org/priestdb/PriestDBbylastName-W.html . Viewed July 2010.

[4] Press release from SNAP: "Sex Abuse Victims 'Outraged' That Bishop Didn't Call Cops, June 22, 2006. http://www.snapnetwork.org/snap_press_releases/2006_press_releases/062206_santa_rosa_bishop_reporting.htm

[5] "Riz Khan – Pope Benedict's Challenge," Al Jazeera English, Season 2010 Ep. 54, April 14, 2010. Interview with the Catholic League's William Donohue and SNAP's David Clohessy. Viewed at http://www.youtube.com/watch?v=44ZHCP6PflE in June of 2010.

[6] Tim Townsend, "Advocate for those abused by priest ramps up since European scandal."

[7] Bruni. Also, "Database of Publicly Accused Priests in the United States," http://www.bishop-accountability.org/priestdb/PriestDBbylastName-C.html . Viewed July 2010.

[8] Dawn Fallik, "Priest scandal puts focus on victims' advocate," St. Louis *Post-Dispatch*, May 12, 2002.

[9] Scott Charton, Associated Press, "Brother pitted against brother over sexual abuse allegations," *Houston Chronicle*, April 13, 2002, p. A27.

[10] Fallik.

[11] Clohessy.

[12] "Association of Community Organizations for Reform Now (ACORN)," DiscoverTheNetworks.org. Viewed from http://www.discoverthenetworks.org/groupProfile.asp?grpid=6968 in June 2010. (A huge amount of information about ACORN and their activities is available at this site.)

[13] Ibid.

[14] Saul D. Alinsky, *Rules for Radicals* (New York: Random House, 1971).

[15] Ibid.

[16] *Association of Community Organizations for Reform Now a/k/a ACORN, and David Clohessy, Appellants, v. St. Louis County*, No. 89-3011. United States Court of Appeals, Eighth Circuit. Submitted Nov. 14, 1990. Decided April 8, 1991.

[17] "Remarks at Palm Sunday Mass," Archdiocese of New York press release, March 28, 2010. Viewed at http://www.archny.org/news-events/news-press-releases/index.cfm?i=15982
in June 2010.

[18] "Clergy sex victims blast NY Archbishop Dolan," SNAP press release, March 29, 2010. Viewed at http://www.snapnetwork.org/snap_statements/2010_statements/032910_clergy_sex_victims_blast_ny_archbishop_dolan.htm in June 2010.

[19] Alinsky.

[20] Manya A. Brachear, "More priests likely to sue: Clerics say court is only defense," December 3, 2006.

[21] "Letter to Rudy Giuliani," Survivors Network of those Abused by Priests, January 25, 2008. Viewed at http://www.snapnetwork.org/snap_letters/2008_letters/012508_giuliani_placa_plea.html

11

No Good Deed ...

One of the most enduring traits of SNAP is their sheer and determined unwillingness to acknowledge the dedicated efforts in recent years by the Catholic Church in the United States to combat child sexual abuse.

SNAP's hatred for Church leaders is unwavering.

Take the organization's approach to the Archdiocese of Los Angeles.

Even by his own admission, Cardinal Roger Mahony made some poor decisions in handling some abuse cases. Tragically, despite being one of the first bishops in the country to establish measures and protocols to address abusive priests, his efforts were not fully adequate, and minors were harmed. He has since apologized publicly on numerous occasions. However, more importantly, Cardinal Mahony, as the shepherd for the nation's largest archdiocese, has supervised a number of important actions dedicated to help grieving victims and protect children from further abuse. Under Cardinal Mahony's jurisdiction, the Los Angeles archdiocese:

- has paid over $720 million in settlements to help give victims the help they need;
- has trained more than 100,000 clergy, staff, volunteers, and parents in the much-heralded VIRTUS[1] sex abuse awareness program;
- has trained over 200,000 children in the "Good-Touch / Bad-Touch"[2] program to educate them of child abuse and how to report it;
- has fingerprinted and/or administered a thorough background check for every priest, deacon, teacher, and volunteer before working with children;
- instituted the Sexual Abuse Advisory Board;
- created the Office of Victims Assistance Ministry to "help abused victims find healing"; and
- formed the Office of Safeguard the Children and overseen the formation of Safeguard the Children parish committees.[3]

Experts in the field of child abuse will tell you that these measures are exactly what an organization needs to do to protect children and create a safe environment for kids.

Yet, apparently, none of this has meant anything to SNAP. In the eyes of the group, the Church still functions as it did 40 years ago. Here is what Joelle Casteix, the agitated "Southwest Director" of SNAP, said as recently as April of 2010:

> "Cardinal Mahony and his team do not care about children's safety."[4]

Good grief. In addition to the measures above, Cardinal Mahony has made it a policy to personally meet privately with any abuse victim who desires to do so. In many instances, the individual is quite belligerent with the Cardinal, even though the archbishop may have had nothing to do with the priest or the abuse. If part of the healing process for a victim entails screaming at a Cardinal, then that is something the Church must be willing to accept. Unless one has been a victim of such awful abuse himself, one cannot understand the deep pain and anger that such an individual has experienced.

But it seems hardly fair for SNAP to claim that the Cardinal "doesn't care" about the welfare of children in light of the many efforts he has made to safeguard kids. (Before entering the priesthood, Cardinal Mahony's focus was in social work. He obtained a master's degree in the subject from Catholic University.)

Notably, an important result of the proactive measures that Cardinal Mahony oversaw has been that only *one* archdiocean priest in all of Los Angeles has been accused of contemporaneously abusing a minor since the year 2000.[5] Almost all allegations that accusers make against priests today go back several years, usually decades. Compare that record with that of the Los Angeles Unified School District, and one can see that the Catholic Church in Los Angeles is *by far* a safer place for children.

Has the Church's efforts to rectify its past progressed perfectly? Of course not.

But consider: Since the start of the abuse crisis, the Catholic Church in the United States:

- o has paid over $2 billion in legal settlements to those claiming abuse by priests;
- o has paid for over $69 million in therapy to victims;

- has instituted a "zero tolerance" policy in which any credibly accused priest is immediately removed from ministry. Law enforcement is also notified;
- has trained nearly 6 million children in giving them skills to protect them from abuse (via programs such as "Good-Touch / Bad-Touch"[6] and "Touching Safety"[7]);
- has trained over 2 million adults, including 99 percent of all priests, in recognizing signs of abuse;
- has conducted over 2 million background checks, including those in the intensified screening process for aspiring seminarians and priests;
- has installed "Victim Assistance Coordinators" in every diocese, "assuring victims that they will be heard"; and
- has conducted audits of *every* diocese to ensure full implementation of the June 2002 *Charter for the Protection of Children and Young People*, a comprehensive set of procedures established by the bishops "to [address] allegations of sexual abuse of minors by Catholic clergy. The Charter also includes guidelines for reconciliation, healing, accountability, and prevention of further acts of abuse."[8,9]

The result of these measures is that there has been a remarkably dramatic reduction in reported cases of abuse by Catholic clergy. In 2009 there were only six reported allegations against priests in the United States contemporaneously abusing a minor.

Yet none of these measures have apparently meant anything to SNAP.

No Good Deed ...

In March of 2010, Barbara Dorris, SNAP's "Outreach Director," wrote in a press statement, "The church's deeply-rooted, long-standing and widespread cover up of horrific child sex crimes demands broad structural reform."[10]

Dorris' remark is very revealing. In the wake of all the measures the Church has taken, her comment implies that SNAP's crusade may extend beyond the mere desire for justice and healing for victims. Rather, SNAP demands "structural reform" from the Catholic Church. (One cannot help but notice the gall in telling another organization how to structure itself, especially when it comes to a 2,000-year-old organization like the Catholic Church, instituted by Jesus Christ himself.)

What sort of "structural reform" does Dorris propose? Dorris did not elaborate. Unfortunately, "structural reform" is often a code phrase for "women priests," married priests, and the abolition of the celibacy requirement. Indeed, a 2003 position paper by SNAP listed "not ordaining women" and "celibacy" as "Key Components" in their gripes about the Catholic Church.[11]

NOTES AND REFERENCES

[1] The National Catholic Risk Retention Group, Inc., VIRTUS, www.virtus.org

[2] Childhelp, the "Good-Touch/Bad-Touch" curriculum. The name "Good-Touch/Bad-Touch" is copyrighted and trademarked by Childhelp, www.childhelp.org

[3] "Our Children Are Our Most Valuable Treasure" (pamphlet), Archdiocese of Los Angeles, 2008. See also: www.la-archdiocese.org/protecting/index.php

[4] SNAP press release, "Abuse Victims to Leaflet Parish Where Accused Cleric Will Work," April 2010. Downloaded from http://www.snapnetwork.org/snap_press_releases/2010_press_releases/041110_abuse_victims_to_leaflet_parish_where_accused_cleric_will_work.htm in May 2010.

[5] Sheila McNiff, "Patterns of abuse," *Los Angeles Times*, December 16, 2007. Not included in this count are the 4-5 extern and religious order priests who have been accused in which the alleged abuse occurred since 2000.

[6] The National Catholic Risk Retention Group, Inc., "Touching Safety Program," www.virtus.org

[7] Childhelp, the "Good-Touch/Bad-Touch" curriculum. The name "Good-Touch/Bad-Touch" is copyrighted and trademarked by Childhelp, www.childhelp.org

[8] Center for Applied Research in the Apostolate, "2009 Survey of Allegations and Costs: A Summary Report for the Secretariat of Child and Youth Protection, United States Conference of Catholic Bishops."

[9] United States Conference of Catholic Bishops (USCCB), "Charter for the Protection of Children and Young People: Essential Norms: Statement of Episcopal Commitment," Revised June 2005.

[10] SNAP press statement, "SNAP statement on Cardinal Brady," March 18, 2010. Downloaded from http://www.snapnetwork.org/snap_statements/2010_statements/031810_snap_statement_on_cardinal_brady.htm in May 2010.

[11] Survivors Network of Those Abused by Priests, "Sexual Abuse and the Catholic Church: The Need for Federal Intervention," November 2003 position paper.

Times Have Changed

"No one would hold a brain surgeon to today's standard of care for professional decisions he made in 1970. Yet the decisions made in 1970 by Catholic bishops, who routinely consulted with mental health professionals about sick priests, are being judged by today's standards." – Attorney Martin Nussbaum, October 2006.[1]

It must be repeated that nothing can mitigate the devastating harm that Catholic priests committed upon innocent youth. Their criminal abuse ravaged families and extinguished their faith. Nothing can vanish this truth.

With that said, counselor Nussbaum is correct. The Church is being unfairly criticized for a standard that did not exist at the time that the majority of abuse is alleged to have occurred; that is, the mid-1960's to the early 1980's.[2]

In her March 2009 address to the Irish Bishop's Conference about the lessons learned from the abuse crisis in the United States, Dr. Monica Applewhite also discussed the history in the United States of dealing with sex offenders. Responding to a series of high-profile sexually motivated murders, legislators in the 1930's and 1940's passed laws to confront "sexual psychopaths."[3] Surprising to us today, rather than prison sentences, treatment-based sentences were enacted for sex offenders. An offender went to treatment until he was "cured"; that is, until the offender "showed remorse, took responsibility for the offense and agreed not to do it again."[4]

> "From the 1950's to the 1980's, these treatment-based interventions for sexual criminals were not only enormously prevalent in the United States, but surveys of ordinary citizens showed that they were enormously popular."[5]

Dr. Applewhite added,

> "[T]he science of human sexuality and sexual offending is extraordinarily young. Virtually all of the information we utilize today regarding the treatment and supervision of sexual offenders has been discovered since 1985."[6]

Yet many in the media continue to blast Catholic Church officials for how they handled abusive priests in their ranks decades ago.

While it is a tragic truth that Catholic priests wrecked terrible harm on youngsters, it is also a sad and inescapable fact that treatment was the prevailing approach to dealing with abusers decades ago. During the 1970's, when the Church was sending priests to treatment, "the criminal justice system was doing the very same thing with convicted offenders – sending them to treatment instead of prison," says Dr. Applewhite.[7]

Now we know better.

Times Have Changed

But questions remain: Why does the media rarely acknowledge these facts? While the media has no problem chasing down priests who may have abused decades ago, why do they not confront judges and doctors? Weren't they the ones who failed to protect children and allowed molesters to avoid punishment and prison?

NOTES AND REFERENCES

[1] L. Martin Nussbaum, "Changing the rules: Selective justice for Catholic institutions," *America*, May 15, 2006.

[2] John Jay College of Criminal Justice, "The Nature and Scope of the Problem of Sexual Abuse of Minors by Catholic Priests and Deacons in the United States," 2004.

[3] "Address of Dr. Monica Applewhite to the Irish Bishops, March 10, 2009," The National Board for Safeguarding Children in the Catholic Church (Ireland).

[4] Ibid.

[5] Ibid.

[6] Ibid.

[7] Tim Drake, "Change in Vatican Culture: A Sex Abuse Expert Sees Hope in Pope Benedict" National Catholic Register, April 25-May 8, 2010 issue.

13

Working the Pews

As the media frenzy reached its height in the spring of 2002 and big-money settlements were clearly on the horizon, a man serving time in Corcoran State Prison in California's Central Valley (also home to murderers Charles Manson and Phil Spector) wrote to the Los Angeles archdiocese. The convict claimed abuse from not just one, but two, priests. His first claim was that priest Fr. Edward Dober "tightly hugged" him during the 1990-1991 school year, when he was a student at Our Lady Queen of Angels Seminary.[1] Faced with the charge, the archdiocese investigated the allegation. A retired FBI agent and the Clergy Misconduct Oversight Board, which Cardinal Mahony had formed several years earlier, looked into the claims. A few months later, the board found absolutely "no credibility to the claim."[2] With no other allegations ever filed against him, Fr. Dober continued in ministry.

Even though an investigation exonerated the priest of the flimsy charge of "tightly hugging" someone in the early 1990's, the army of SNAP went on the attack. In early 2004, members of the group summoned the media and descended upon Dober's parish in Paramount, California, during Sunday Mass. They passed out yellow flyers to inform churchgoers that the priest had been accused of "sexual abuse of a minor."[3] It's doubtful that the flyers said that the "sexual abuse" was the claim of a "tight hug" from a felon serving a lengthy sentence in one of California's notorious prisons. It's also doubtful that the flyer said anything about the charge being investigated and found false.

With a number of supportive media gathered, an irate SNAP spokesperson angrily complained, "I am outraged that the church, at this late date, is still placing priority on protecting priests."[4]

SNAP also failed to inform the public that the prisoner at Corcoran State Prison did not just accuse Fr. Dober of abuse. The man also claimed that yet *another* priest, Fr. Richard Martini, had "fondled" him during a water polo event during the same year at the same school that Fr. Dober "tightly hugged" him.

Again, as with the Fr. Dober case, investigators found the case against Fr. Martini to be totally unfounded. In fact, the accusation was "unsupported even by the accuser's own witnesses."[5]

As they did with Fr. Dober, the fearless SNAP continued to hound the innocent Fr. Martini. Years later, in 2010, when the priest, now a monsignor, was transferred to a parish in northwest Los Angeles County, some parents became concerned when they learned that their new pastor had been accused of molestation. SNAP saw that this was a great situation on which to capitalize.

Similar to the Dober protest six years earlier, they took the approach of handing out flyers at Monsignor Martini's new assignment "warning" the parish of the cleric. This time, SNAP recruited unknowing parishioners into helping them with the task. Again, it's unlikely that

SNAP's flyers honestly informed parishioners that the "abuse" charge originated from a convicted felon and that the old allegation was found to be baseless. It's also unlikely that SNAP's flyers honestly informed its recipients that the inmate had also accused another priest of "sexual abuse" with the shaky charge that the cleric had "tightly hugged" him.

SNAP reached yet another height of feverishness. SNAP's Joelle Casteix cried about the situation, "The Archdiocese is telling parishioners that their kids' safety is far less important than the reputation of a priest."[6]

SNAP's Casteix also totally mislead people by saying in a press release that the priest was "credibly accused in a court of law."[7] In fact, there was not any criminal case against Richard Martini – nor has there ever been one in his life.[8]

In addition, Casteix claimed that Father Martini was "found liable" of wrongdoing.[9] This was false also.[10]

Unfortunately, one can readily see that impartiality and fairness are not part of SNAP's approach.

On another note, the exonerations had no effect on the prisoner's determination to maintain his civil lawsuits against the archdiocese. Because of a California law that lifted the statute of limitations for accusers to sue the Church (SB 1779, see pp. 116-118), there was absolutely nothing the archdiocese could do to halt *anyone* from suing them, even if the claim was found to be false. The archdiocese faced a sudden avalanche of hundreds of cases, and it was literally impossible to litigate them all. They had little choice but to "bundle" the lawsuits into global, "blanket" settlements. The result for the inmate was that he received a healthy share of a $60 million settlement in December 2006 with 44 other plaintiffs. Perseverance certainly paid off for this prisoner. Neither Dober nor Martini wanted their cases to be part of the settlement, but since the inmate sued the archdiocese, rather than the priests themselves, there was not a lot the clerics could do except maintain their innocence.[11] The archdiocese felt compelled to settle the suits because a number of serious and substantiated abuse cases were involved.[12]

Joe Maher, the president of Opus Bono Sacerdotii has observed the problems that large-scale "blanket" settlements have wrought. "Once the lawsuits are paid, everyone assumes the priests are guilty," Maher has said. "If you think it's tough proving an allegation from 30 years back, try disproving it."[13]

NOTES AND REFERENCES

[1] "Addendum to the Report to the People of God," Archdiocese of Los Angeles, October 12, 2005. Downloaded from http://www.bishop-accountability.org/usccb/natureandscope/dioceses/reports/losangelesca_addendum.htm in June 2010.

[2] Chad Greene, "Anti-abuse activists protest at church," Long Beach *Press-Telegram* (CA), February 9, 2004, A2.

[3] Ibid.

[4] Marianne Love, "Abuse claim haunts pastor," *The Signal*, April 8, 2010.

[5] "An Open Letter from the Archdiocese of Los Angeles to the People of Santa Clarita concerning Msgr. Richard Martini," The Tidings, April 9, 2010.

[6] SNAP press release, "Abuse Victims to Leaflet Parish Where Accused Cleric Will Work," April 2010. Downloaded from http://www.snapnetwork.org/snap_press_releases/2010_press_releases/041110

_abuse_victims_to_leaflet_parish_where_accused_cleric_will_work.htm in May 2010.

[7] Ibid.

[8] Ibid.

[9] "An Open Letter from the Archdiocese of Los Angeles to the People of Santa Clarita concerning Msgr. Richard Martini."

[10] The inmate filed his suit *against the archdiocese* (not Martini himself) in a civil court, and lawyers reached a settlement. There was never any verdict in the suit. In fact, "[t]he negotiated settlement [did] not include any admission of liability on the part of the church," reported the *Los Angeles Times*. (John Spano, Paul Pringle and Jean Guccione, "Church To Settle With 45 Accusers," *Los Angeles Times*, December 02, 2006.)

[11] "An Open Letter from the Archdiocese of Los Angeles to the People of Santa Clarita concerning Msgr. Richard Martini."

[12] Ibid.

[13] Kim Ode, "Attorney gaining a worldwide reputation for his battle against sexually abusive priests," *Star Tribune* (Minneapolis), May 5, 2010.

14

Attorney Jeff Anderson

> "We got a new law passed in California that opens up the statute of limitations for all victims of sexual abuse. It's something we've been trying to do in several states for years. And I'm not waiting for it to click in. I'm suing the sh** out of [the Catholic Church] everywhere: in Sacramento, in Santa Clara, in Santa Rosa, in San Francisco, in Oakland, in L.A., and everyplace else."
> – Attorney Jeff Anderson, April 2003 interview[1]

Meet Minneapolis attorney Jeff Anderson.

No single individual has gone after the Catholic Church more than Anderson has. It's estimated that he's earned hundreds of millions of dollars suing the Catholic Church.[2]

How has Anderson prevailed?

In an April 2010 newspaper profile, attorney Jeff Anderson told the *Washington Post*, "I believe Christ was a student of Buddha."[3]

What at first blush appears to be an innocuous remark actually tells a lot about Jeff Anderson. He never lets the facts get in the way of what he wants to believe. (There's not even the slightest shred of evidence, for example, that Jesus was a "student of Buddha.")

For years, Anderson has been screaming of an "international criminal conspiracy"[4] by the Vatican to cover up the awful sex abuse of children. Yet, like with his remark about Jesus and Buddha, there's never been any support for the claim.

Sadly, many in the media have uncritically eaten up the wild claims by Anderson.

Even the liberal Minneapolis weekly *City Pages* has likened Anderson to a "wisecracking ambulance chaser with a reputation for hunting priests and an advanced degree in self-promotion."[5]

An early case for Anderson as a lawyer was defending gay activists after police raids of bathhouses. He also defended a homeless man for indecent exposure in a church basement.

In looking back on his early lawsuits against the Church, Anderson's wife confides, "[I]t was more about the flash and the appearance of it all. He liked to play the part of the scrappy little lawyer, a down-and-dirty sort of a--hole. He was an actor on a stage. And he was very good at commanding an audience."[6]

Anderson's *modus operandi* is easy to identify: Get out in front of a lot of cameras and make a lot of noise. Say whatever it takes. The facts don't matter.

And there's little doubt that newspaper journalists love Jeff Anderson. "He's everything you want an attorney to be if you're a reporter," Matt Carroll, a columnist for the *Boston Globe*, has said. "He has lots of information, he returns your phone calls, and he has good quotes ... [A]nytime I need big-picture type comments, I give him a call."[7]

Intimidation also appears to be part of Anderson's repertoire. Upon filing a lawsuit, Anderson has been known to place a bullying phone call to the accused priest. "They usually don't answer," Anderson has said. "But if they don't, they'll see it on their caller ID, or get my message. And they'll know I am on to them."[8] One wonders what the Minnesota Office of Lawyers Responsibility Board would say about such a tawdry tactic.

"Innocent until proven guilty" is not a belief that Anderson appears to subscribe to. Joe Maher, president of Opus Bono Sacerdotii, told Minneapolis' *City Pages* weekly newspaper, "Civil attorneys like Jeff Anderson have a responsibility to look at each individual and make a determination, an authentic determination – to find out whether or not an accusation has merit before they file a suit. And it's already impossible to do that. They meet with someone for a few minutes, lump allegations together, throw lawsuits at the wall, and see what sticks. In the meantime, men's lives are being ruined. They don't care. And if they say they know that everyone they have targeted is guilty, they're lying to you or to themselves."[9]

"When attorneys go to the media with this stuff now, everyone they sue is guilty until proven innocent, and that's neither just nor fair," said Maher.[10]

In June 2007, a Chicago-area priest who says he was falsely accused by a client of Anderson filed a defamation lawsuit against his accuser. An angry Anderson placed a call to Cardinal Francis George and pressed him to get the lawsuit dropped. When the Cardinal refused, Anderson huffed and cooked up his next maneuver. "I want a lawsuit filed Wednesday," ordered Anderson, "and I want to name Cardinal George personally for his failure to protect these victims."[11] In this case, it appears a simple refusal of his demand was worthy of a fresh, new lawsuit against the Church.

In an interview setting, Anderson is especially frustrating and problematic. When espousing on "canon law" or "Church teaching," Anderson's sober demeanor and tone lead people to believe that he is being truthful and actually knowledgeable of what he's talking about. Usually the interviewer is completely unschooled in Catholic teaching, and the journalist just takes what Anderson says at face value. But the bottom line is that all too often Anderson either flat-out lies to his interviewer or is completely erroneous.

Here is an example of a typical Anderson interview. In April of 2010, Anderson appeared on the left-wing political program *Democracy Now*, hosted by socialist Amy Goodman. When addressing the issue of how the Church handles abusive priests, Anderson said the following:

> ... [Priests] are required to by their superiors, from the bishop to the Vatican, to keep [abuse] secret. And that's under protocols and laws developed by the Pontiff, by the Vatican that says "We are required to avoid scandal, to protect the reputation of the church" and in so doing, are embedded with an ethos, a norm that says, we move the priest, avoid scandal, do not report it to anybody outside the clerical culture, and continue to move and protect the priest without regard to the well-being of the children ... [N]othing has really fundamentally changed in the clerical culture. And that the decision of the Pontiff and at the Vatican, they're fundamentally still operating under the same protocols of secrecy and self-protection that they did 100 years ago.[12]

It cannot be overstated how false Anderson's words are. His claims could not be further from the truth. If Anderson were making his assertions in the year 1960, he might actually have a leg to stand on. But, again, he said this in April of 2010.

The fact is that is the well-established policy in the United States for Church officials to immediately report credible child abuse accusations to civil authorities. Anderson should already know this.

Here is Article Four of the *Charter for the Protection of Children and Young People* from the United States Conference of Catholic Bishops. Based on principles and policies from years earlier, the charter was approved in June of 2002.

> ARTICLE 4. Dioceses/eparchies are to report an allegation of sexual abuse of a person who is a minor to the public authorities. Dioceses/ eparchies are to comply with all applicable civil laws with respect to the reporting of allegations of sexual abuse of minors to civil authorities and cooperate in their investigation in accord with the law of the jurisdiction in question.
>
> Dioceses/eparchies are to cooperate with public authorities about reporting cases even when the person is no longer a minor.[13]

Then there's Article Five:

> ARTICLE 5. We affirm the words of His Holiness, Pope John Paul II, in his Address to the Cardinals of the United States and Conference Officers: "There is no place in the priesthood or religious life for those who would harm the young."
>
> Sexual abuse of a minor by a cleric is a crime in the universal law of the Church (CIC, c. 1395 §2; CCEO, c. 1453 §1). Because of the seriousness of this matter, jurisdiction has been reserved to the Congrega-

tion for the Doctrine of the Faith (*Motu proprio Sacramentorum sanctitatis tutela*, AAS 93, 2001).

Sexual abuse of a minor is also a crime in all civil jurisdictions in the United States. Diocesan/eparchial policy is to provide that for even a single act of sexual abuse of a minor —whenever it occurred— which is admitted or established after an appropriate process in accord with canon law, the offending priest or deacon is to be permanently removed from ministry and, if warranted, dismissed from the clerical state.[14]

In other words, the policies of United States bishops are the exact opposite of what Anderson claims they are. The *Charter* outlines policy for *all* of the Catholic Church in the United States.

There's no other reasonable conclusion to reach except that Anderson flat-out lied in the interview. The 2002 charter was a well-publicized and transformative measure by the Church to combat child sexual abuse and address the problem of abusive priests. Many heralded its "zero tolerance" policy to child abuse. Anderson surely heard about all of this.

Conclusion: Honesty is not a quality to find in Jeff Anderson.

(By the way, many of the measures of the 2002 *Charter* were already in practice a decade earlier. In 1992, U.S. bishops publicly endorsed its "Five Principles" in responding to abuse claims. These principles were articulated five years earlier, in 1987. They included immediately removing an accused priest from ministry and complying with civil laws in promptly reporting abuse to authorities.[15])

In addition, it appears that Anderson's thirst for "flash and appearance" often pushes aside principles. For example, Anderson proudly trumpets himself as a member of the American Civil Liberties Union (ACLU). That anyone who claims to fight for the welfare of children and against child abuse would stand with the ACLU is troubling. The ACLU has adamantly fought efforts to shield children from pornography in public libraries. Its members have argued that distribution and possession of child pornography should not be a crime.[16] Members have also argued against record-keeping requirements for porn filmmakers to make sure all actors are of legal age.[17]

The ACLU has also defended an awful organization called the North American Man-Boy Love Association (NAMBLA). NAMBLA has advocated, among other things, the removal of age of consent laws, and they have argued that children have every right to consent to sex with whomever they want.[18]

Anderson champions himself as a "crusader" for children, but he aligns himself with an organization that's anything but that. Why?

In discussing his practice of suing the Church, Anderson is yet another litigator who has aired the common line, "It's not about the money." Yet his own words and actions suggest otherwise. Anderson has openly admitted that at the start of his career as a public defender, "People would walk into my office and say, 'I have a problem.' I'd say, 'How much money do you have?'"[19]

In January of 2010 Anderson launched what he calls his "Child Porn Initiative." In a press conference to announce the enterprise, Anderson announced that he would be "going after" those who indulge in child pornography. It is a very noble effort, indeed. But how would Anderson do this? By using some of his hundreds of millions of dollars he's gathered to support the many organizations that successfully combat these awful Internet crimes? By setting up a fund to help needy children who have been so horribly victimized by child pornography?

No. It appears that only the lure of money attracted Anderson to the cause. In announcing the launch of his new pursuit, Anderson said he had "recently learned" of a federal law passed *four years earlier* which allows those depicted in child pornography to sue those who possess or trade their unlawful images. The minimal claim, according to "Masha's Law," would be $150,000 per violation.[20] With the 25% to 40% contingency fee that Anderson is estimated to collect, that's a *minimum* of $37,500 to $60,000 per violation in his pocket. So it seems that only when Anderson saw an opportunity to profit off the repulsive crime of child pornography did he take a serious interest in pursuing it.

"It's not about the money"? Judging from Anderson's own behavior, that seems hard to believe.

SB 1779: How lawyers worked the California legislature to target the Catholic Church

As the scandals erupted in Boston in 2002 and seemed to grow exponentially by the day, veteran litigants like Jeff Anderson went into action.

The big fish was California, home to over 10 million Catholics and the deep pockets of several dioceses. The biggest, of course, was Los Angeles.

But there was one pesky barrier between lawyers and their desired treasures. A legal principle called the statute of limitations. How could lawyers take advantage of the growing public anger of the scandals and sue the Catholic Church for big bucks when so many years had passed since the alleged abuses?

Enter the novel idea of California Senate Bill 1779 (SB 1779). With help from members of SNAP, veteran lawyers petitioned lawmakers to craft a law that would lift the statute of limitations of abuse claims. For the calendar year 2003 it allowed any individual to recover damages for childhood sexual abuse, no matter how long ago the alleged abuse supposedly took place. As with all lawsuits of this nature, public institutions, such as public schools, were exempt from the law.

As SB 1779 began working its way into law, lawmakers seemed to forget why the statutes of limitations were in place to begin with. How can any individual defend himself against an emotionally charged claim of child abuse that is said to have happened decades ago? Exculpatory evidence, such as written schedules and verifiable witnesses, often no longer exist. And because of the visceral nature of the allegation, the accused individual is at an inherent and unfair disadvantage.

The proponents of SB 1779 tried to claim that the bill was not designed to target the Catholic Church, but this assertion was disingenuous. Jeff Anderson and Laurence Drivon, who had extensive experience suing the Church, helped craft the bill. They were then called as "technical experts" during hearings on the proposed legislation.[21] In addition, during discussions of the bill, lawmakers *only* heard from individuals who claimed to have been abused by clergy.[22]

Meanwhile, the author of the bill, state senator John L. Burton, a Democrat from San Francisco, said his bill clearly focused "at deep pocket defendants such as the

Catholic Church."[23] And Burton's own press secretary admitted that the bill was prompted by calls to their office from people who claimed to have been molested by Catholic priests.[24]

And lest there be any doubt about the intention of SB 1779, here was attorney Jeff Anderson shortly after the law was passed:

"We got a new law passed in California that opens up the statute of limitations for all victims of sexual abuse. It's something we've been trying to do in several states for years. And I'm not waiting for it to click in. I'm suing the shit out of [the Catholic Church] everywhere: in Sacramento, in Santa Clara, in Santa Rosa, in San Francisco, in Oakland, in L.A., and everyplace else."[25]

Notice how Anderson said, "*We* got a new law passed"; not, "California passed" or "The people of California passed." The true target of SB 1779 was undoubtedly the Catholic Church.

According to SB 1779, "the target of the lawsuits could not be an alleged abuser but only an employer or other responsible third party who knew or should have known of the abuse and failed to take reasonable steps to prevent it."[26] That's what the law said, but the reality was something entirely different. Whether or not the Church "knew or should have known of the abuse" or "failed to take reasonable steps to prevent it" became completely irrelevant. Any "credible" claim of abuse – no matter how long ago or obtuse – became eligible for a lawsuit.

Attorney Jeff Anderson

NOTES AND REFERENCES

[1] David Schimke, "True Believer: Paul Attorney Jeff Anderson has already made millions 'suing the sh**' out of the Catholic Church. Now all he wants is another reformation and a little credit for time served," *City Pages* (MN), April 16, 2003.

[2] It has been widely reported that in 2002 Anderson conceded that he had made $60 million suing the Church. That was before several large, high-profile settlements, including the $720 million in settlements paid out in Los Angeles in 2006 and 2007.

[3] Peter Slevin, "Jeff Anderson, jousting with the Vatican from a small law office in St. Paul," *Washington Post*, April 19, 2010.

[4] For example: John Brewer, "St. Paul attorney ignites latest priest abuse furor," *Pioneer Press* (MN), March 25, 2010.

[5] Schimke.

[6] Ibid.

[7] Ibid.

[8] Kevin Harter, "Jeff Anderson, Man on a Mission," *Pioneer Press* (MN), January 28, 2007.

[9] Schimke.

[10] Ibid.

[11] Terry Carter, "Collaring the Clergy: Jeffrey Anderson Goes Global with His Pursuit of Pedophiles," *ABA Journal* (MN), June 18, 2007.

[12] Segment from *Democracy Now*, "Attorney Uncovers Docs Implicating Vatican in Sexual Abuse Cover-Up," April 29, 2010. Audio/video available at http://www.democracynow.org/2010/4/29/attorney_uncovers_docs_implicating_vatican_in

[13] United States Conference of Catholic Bishops (USCCB), "Charter for the Protection of Children and Young People: Essential Norms: Statement of Episcopal Commitment," Revised June 2005.

[14] Ibid.

[15] "Address of Dr. Monica Applewhite to the Irish Bishops, March 10, 2009," The National Board for Safeguarding Children in the Catholic Church (Ireland). Also, Susan Hines-Brigger, "Clergy Sex Abuse: Bishop Joseph Galante Responds," *St. Anthony Messenger*, June 2003.

[16] Maggie Mulvihill, "ACLU: New child-porn law won't pass court challenge," *Boston Herald*, December 9, 1997. See also: "ACLU Policy to Legalize Child Porn Distribution," *Stop the ACLU* (web site), http://www.stoptheaclu.com/2005/07/17/aclu-policy-to-legalize-child-porn-distribution/ ACLU

[17] "ACLU Policy to Legalize Child Porn Distribution," *Stop the ACLU* (web site), http://www.stoptheaclu.com/2005/07/17/aclu-policy-to-legalize-child-porn-distribution/ ACLU . Downloaded April 2010.

[18] "ACLU and Nambla: A Match Made in Hell," *Stop the ACLU* (web site), http://www.stoptheaclu.com/2005/06/17/aclu-and-nambla-a-match-made-in-hell/ . Downloaded April 2010.

[19] Schimke.

[20] "Child Pornography Initiative – Masha's Law," www.andersonadvocates.com/ViewFile.aspx?ID=472 (Anderson's web site). Viewed February 2010.

[21] Jack Smith, "Bishops back constitutional challenge to California sex abuse law," Catholic News Service, July 15, 2004.

[22] "Who was the real target of Senate Bill 1779?" *The Tidings*, December 2, 2005.

[23] "News," *Los Angeles Lay Catholic Mission*, June 2002. From http://www.losangelesmission.com/ed/news/0602news.htm

[24] Ibid.

[25] Schimke.

[26] Carl Ingram, "Panel Backs Abuse Case Bill; Legislature: Senate committee OKs measure lengthening statute of limitations on suits against Catholic Church or other third parties," *Los Angeles Times*, May 8, 2002, B1.

15

"Considerable Doubt"

> "People have to come to understand that there is a large scam going on with personal injury attorneys, and what began as a serious effort has now expanded to become a huge money-making proposition." – *Wall Street Journal* writer Dorothy Rabinowitz, April 2005[1]

In November of 2001, two Massachusetts men serving time in the MCI-Shirley prison, Sean Murphy and Byron Worth, pleaded guilty to trying to scam the Archdiocese of Boston out of $850,000. They had claimed that a well-known abuser, former priest John Geoghan, had molested them years earlier when they were youths. They probably would have gotten away with their crime, except Murphy had a lengthy rap sheet, and officials discovered that Murphy and Worth didn't even live in the town when and where they say the abuse occurred. (Even after he was released from jail years later, Murphy continued his life of crime. In addition to being suspected of other thefts, Murphy was notably indicted in 2009 for stealing 27 New York Giants Super Bowl rings.[2])

DOUBLE STANDARD

Around the time that Murphy and Worth were being convicted of their false accusations against the priest, a Boston lawyer reportedly commented on the nature of the case. "I have some contacts in the prison system, having been an attorney for some time, and it has been made known to me that this is a current and popular scam," the counselor said.[3]

The biggest mistake the two con men may have made is that they filed their lawsuit too early. If they had waited a couple of years later, they may have gotten away with their scam. Here's why:

Shortly after the Archdiocese of Boston settled 552 complaints of abuse for $85 million, Daniel Lyons of *Forbes* magazine questioned two leading plaintiff attorneys, Mitchell Garabedian and Roderick MacLeish, Jr. When Lyons questioned them on the veracity of the claims that had been made, both men hinted that some of the accusations may not have been totally legitimate.[4]

Needless to say, many supporters of the Church began to gripe at these new revelations. Lyons quoted William Donohue of the Catholic League, "For them to come out now and play this card shows how dishonest the process has been from the beginning."[5]

In 2004, the *Boston Phoenix* published a similar narrative. Columnist Harvey Silverglate reported, "There is considerable doubt about the veracity of many of the new claims, quite a few of which were made after it became apparent that the Church was willing to settle sex-abuse cases for big bucks."[6] (By the way, while the *Boston Globe* gets the most accolades for their 2002 reporting of clergy abuse, it was actually the *Phoenix*, a lesser-known weekly paper, which was heavily riding the story a year earlier.)

The lawyers' admission was particularly frustrating. Plaintiff attorneys regularly griped to the media when the

"Considerable Doubt"

Boston Archdiocese wanted to question the legitimacy of some of the accusations before handing over a sizable amount of money.[7] Lawyers such as California's John Manly have accused the Church of "running over" their clients during depositions.[8] Yet depositions usually just consist of questioning accusers about the nature of the abuse and noting any inconsistencies that may exculpate a priest.

For Church officials and lawyers, the thinking is logical: If an individual is able make the step of going to an attorney and describing his abuse in order to file a lawsuit, surely this same person can answer some questions from the very organization that's cutting the checks.

Unfortunately, many lawyers have been adamant that their clients receive settlements with "no questions asked." They have forcefully claimed, "People don't make this stuff up."[9]

Well, to that, one can say that Sean Murphy and Byron Worth definitely *did* make it up.

Are we to believe that they are the only ones?

Some dioceses, meanwhile, have simply decided to take a simple approach when it comes to settling lawsuits against them. In 2002, a New Hampshire diocese faced accusations of abuse from 62 individuals. Rather than spending the time and resources looking into the merits of the cases, "Diocesan officials did not even ask for specifics such as the dates and specific allegations for the claims," New Hampshire's *Union Leader* reported.[10] Getting money from the diocese could not have been any easier for the complainants. It was almost as simple as a trip to an ATM machine.

"Some victims made claims in the past month, and because of the timing of negotiations, gained closure in just a matter of days," reported the *Nashua Telegraph* (N.H.).[11]

"I've never seen anything like it," a pleased, and much richer, plaintiff attorney admitted.[12]

NOTES AND REFERENCES

[1] Daniel Barrick, "Writer takes up convicted priest's case," *Concord Monitor*, April 29, 2005.

[2] Dan O'Brien, "Lynn Super Bowl Ring Thief Linked to False Priest Sexual-abuse Claim," *Daily Item* (MA), January 29, 2009. Downloaded from http://www.bishop-accountability.org/news2009/01_02/2009_01_29_Obrien_LynnSuper.htm in May 2010.

[3] Rev. Gordon J. MacRae, "Sex Abuse and Signs of Fraud," *Catalyst* (published by the Catholic League), November 2005, p.8.

[4] Daniel Lyons, "Clergy Sex Scammers?" *Forbes*, September 24, 2003.

[5] Ibid.

[6] Harvey A. Silverglate, "Fleecing the shepherd: Will the Church settle the sexual-abuse cases this time around?" *Boston Phoenix*, December 10-16, 2004 issue.

[7] Lyons.

[8] Radio interview, "Privacy Piracy," Host Mari Frank, Attorney John C. Manly, KUCI 88.9 FM (CA), December 5, 2007.

[9] Lyons.

[10] Mark Hayward, "NH Diocese Will Pay $5 Million to 62 Victims," *Union Leader* (NH), November 27, 2002. Cited by Rev. MacRae.

"Considerable Doubt"

[11] Albert McKeon, "Settlement Reached in Abuse Claims," *The Telegraph* (Nashua, NH), November 27, 2002. Downloaded from http://www.bishop-accountability.org/news/2002_11_27_McKeon_SettlementReached.htm in March 2010.

[12] Hayward.

16

Deliver Us From Evil

Throwing around "anti-Catholic" accusations has become quite easy and common. It's easy to label something as "anti-Catholic" simply because it portrays the Church in a negative way. However, sometimes a work is so especially rife with falsehoods and dishonesty – literally from start to finish – that it's difficult to tag it as anything but anti-Catholic propaganda.

Such is the case with the "documentary" film, *Deliver Us From Evil*,[1] that Hollywood unleashed on the public in 2006. Indeed, the film chronicled the despicable crimes of a former California priest, pedophile Oliver O'Grady. O'Grady committed evil abominations that wrecked grievous harm on numerous victims. He shattered innocent children and devastated their families. The stories from his victims and their families are truly poignant and incredibly maddening. It cannot be overstated how revolting O'Grady's actions were.

Director/writer Amy Berg certainly had a golden opportunity to showcase an informative look at a serious topic. However, through crafty editing, dishonest interview subjects, and unchecked facts, director Berg instead deceived her audience and took advantage of the emotions of her viewers. The result is simply a wild and irresponsible hit piece in which nearly every male with a collar is portrayed as a pedophiliac demon.

Movie reviewers loved the film. The movie brags that is only one of only a few films to receive a "100% rating" on the "Rotten Tomatoes" movie review site.[2] Hollywood graced it with an Oscar nomination for Best Documentary.

Unfortunately, movie reviewers are rarely, if ever, fact checkers.

Even before the first frame of film was exposed, Berg took a dishonest approach to her project. Berg and her staff approached an elementary school in Ireland under the false pretense that they were filming a documentary on "multiculturalism."[3] (O'Grady was born in Ireland, and he was deported to there in 2001.) Berg wanted to stir the emotions of her audience by filming the pedophile O'Grady leering at small children on a playground and talking about how children sexually arouse him.

To make matters worse, after the school granted her permission, Berg filmed children with their name tags clearly identifiable. A member of Berg's crew later admitted that they neither sought nor were given permission to use pictures of the children.[4] When the filmmakers later informed the school that their footage would be used for a film about O'Grady, the school "categorically refused" the request. So what did Berg do? She used the footage anyway.[5]

Especially slanted were interview segments in the film when they dealt with Church and theological issues. The film includes several troubling interview segments with Fr. Thomas Doyle, a so-called Catholic priest. His presentations on issues such as the structure of the Church (a "monarchy"?), the history of the Church, the role of the laity, the training of seminarians, and the Eucharist are simply wrong and are not in alignment with official Church teaching. For example, Fr. Doyle states that the Church's requirement of celibacy – a big target of the film – "is not justified anywhere in the Gospels or in the life and times and sayings of Christ." Yet the Bible clearly quotes Jesus praising the gift of celibacy in the Gospel of Matthew (Matt. 19:12), and Paul unequivocally *encourages* celibacy in his First Letter to the Corinthians (1 Cor 7). That a man espousing to be a Catholic priest could air such a blatant falsehood (in a "documentary," no less) should be disturbing to any serious Catholic.

Meanwhile, California attorney John Manly airs a number of falsehoods. For example, he claims that the Church teaches, "[I]f you are not in communion with the church you are damned to hell." A cursory look at the Catechism of the Catholic Church, paragraphs 846-848, rebuts this assertion. Meanwhile, the supposed "theologian" of the film, Patrick Wall, doesn't bother correct Manly. This is no surprise, however, because Wall is actually one of his employees.[6]

Amy Berg clearly puts the Catholic Church and its beliefs in her crosshairs.

In the film Berg often interviews O'Grady about his disgraceful crimes inside a church. Berg overlays graphic descriptions of stomach-turning abuse with images of the Mass and other Catholic imagery. The motivation behind this is clear. It is a not-so-subtle attempt to forcefully equate the Catholic faith and Catholic priests with the nauseating crime of pedophilia.

Then there's Berg's dishonest use of editing. A portion of the film features videotaped depositions of the

O'Grady case given by Church officials, including Los Angeles Cardinal Roger Mahony. (Mahony was Bishop of Stockton for a period of time that O'Grady worked there.) A number of lawyers question the Cardinal about the O'Grady case, and Berg craftily cuts off answers, removes sound, and re-frames the screen in order portray Church officials in the worst light imaginable. Anyone who has seen a Michael Moore film should be familiar with these unscrupulous techniques.

For example, Berg features a 1980 letter from the father of an abuse victim written to a Stockton diocese monsignor. When one reads the entire letter (which would be impossible for a viewer in a theater to do), one clearly sees that the major issue of the father's missive was that O'Grady was spending so much time *with his wife*. (The man and his wife were separated.) The man was also angry at O'Grady's dissenting views towards the sacrament of marriage. However, through the use of deceptive framing, Berg craftily highlights a line of the letter in which the father wrote that O'Grady "took our 2-year-old son for a ride."

"Aha!" the film implies. "Here's more evidence that they knew that O'Grady targeted children!"

But the contents, tone, and entirety of the actual letter make no such claim or implication. Berg clearly misleads her viewers.

Another clear target of *Deliver Us From Evil* is Los Angeles Cardinal Roger Mahony. While O'Grady served 21 years in the diocese of Stockton, Mahony was the bishop from 1980 to 1985, a fraction of O'Grady time there. Yet the film deceives viewers into believing that just about all of O'Grady's disgusting abuse happened under his watch. Two of the adult women featured in the film tell harrowing stories of child sex abuse by O'Grady. While the film bends over backwards to connect Mahony to this abuse, a study of their cases reveals that the incidents took place before Mahony even arrived in Stockton.

In another portion of the film, a series of interview subjects air their frustrations that O'Grady was allowed to continue as a priest. Then Berg places an ominous graphic and caption on the screen: "1982: Roger Mahony moves Oliver O'Grady to another parish 52 miles away." The clear implication is that Mahony surreptitiously "shuffled" the molester O'Grady off to another unsuspecting parish. Although the film suggests otherwise, the movie fails to note that during Mahony's entire tenure in Stockton, *not a single victim or family member* came to him to complain of child abuse by O'Grady.[7]

In fact, the film also fails to disclose that during his tenure in Stockton, then-Bishop Mahony removed the faculties and assignments of two priests in his diocese who were accused of child abuse. It's no surprise that director/writer Berg left out this key fact. It would rebut her implication that Mahony let molesters "run wild" under his care.

Even the simplest statements presented in the film are problematic. Berg published several falsehoods on the screen that appear as captions:

o *"Over 100,000 victims of clergy sexual abuse have come forward in the United States alone"*: The 2004 John Jay study, the most comprehensive study ever done on the issue of Catholic cleric abuse in the United States, found that only one tenth of that number, 10,667, have made such allegations. And the study included all accusations going back to 1950, a period of over a half a century. And in that same period, there were less than 110,000 men serving as Catholic priests in the U.S. For the film's outrageous claim to be true, there would be one victim for nearly every priest who ever served in that period. Berg's claim is preposterous for sure.[8]

o *"President Bush granted the Pope immunity from prosecution"*: President Bush didn't "grant" anybody anything. The United States has recognized the Holy See as a state since 1984. As the head of state, the Pope cannot be called to a trial in another country in the same way that a lawyer in another country cannot simply call in our President. Heads of state have immunity.

o *"Oliver O'Grady is still roaming free in Ireland"*: The claim on its surface is true, but the implication is that the Church should have an eye on him. The truth is that the Church laicized O'Grady. (It means that he is no longer a priest, that the Church made him a regular citizen. This is a common request by abuse victims.) The Church has no oversight over O'Grady than it has over any other private citizen in its country. The fact that O'Grady is "roaming free in Ireland" should be a criticism of the Irish government.

o *"Cardinal Roger Mahony is still in office fighting sexual abuse allegations against 556 priests in his (Los Angeles) diocese"*: "556"? Try 254, less than half of Berg's claim. And those were 254 priests with accusations dating back *to 1930*. Nearly thirty percent of the 254 priests were *deceased* at the time of their accusation.[9]

o *"The Catholic Church declined to be interviewed for this documentary"*: If the topic of the film weren't so sickening, this line would be comical. "The Catholic Church"? "Declined"? Reviewer Grant

Gallicho for Religion News Service rightly asked, "Which part?" The Pope? A cardinal? A bishop? Amy Berg doesn't tell us. Gallicho asked the chairwoman of the Church's national lay review board, which has spent as much time as anybody addressing abuse cases, if filmmakers had contacted the group. They had not.[10] But judging from the final product of the film, any Church officials would surely have been portrayed unfairly and in the most unflattering way.

Yet probably the most unprincipled contrivance in the film is when the filmmakers and their accomplice, Fr. Thomas Doyle, cajole now-adult victims of O'Grady into thinking that they can travel to the Vatican uninvited and meet Church "hierarchy" (the Pope, maybe?). Preying on the terrible pain and awful abuse that O'Grady caused, director Berg and Fr. Doyle lead the victims into thinking that they could simply write a letter to the Vatican, show up at the front doors, and possibly meet the Holy Father. Needless to say, this doesn't happen. The film catalogs the disappointment, and the victims are pained even further.

This is Hollywood exploitation at its ugliest. As a Catholic priest, Fr. Doyle would know more than anyone that citizens cannot merely show up at the Vatican without an appointment and meet high-level administrators. This would be about as likely as walking up to the White House uninvited, being escorted inside, and being able to meet with the Vice President. When Doyle's maneuver fails, he claims that the Church "rejected [the victims]," "abused them," and "[made] them out to be enemies of the Church."

The obvious goal of Berg was to anger viewers further in their distaste for the Catholic Church for "turning away" abuse victims. But any clear-thinking viewer would direct his or her anger at Berg for exploiting people's hopes, vulnerabilities, and pains.

By the way, television network CNN was also there at the Vatican to chronicle Berg and Doyle's failed scheme. (The film includes part of a sympathetic segment from *Paula Zahn Now*.) How did CNN get involved? Simple. Director/writer Amy Berg worked at CNN.

Again, it cannot be emphasized how much of an abomination the crimes of Oliver O'Grady were. He is a disgrace in every sense of the word. The damage he induced is truly incalculable.

It is unfortunate, however, that Amy Berg resorted to such a dishonest approach to her film.

The truth about the condoms, AIDS, and Africa

For the last several years, many have argued that the Catholic Church forbidding the use of condoms is fostering the spread of AIDS in Africa.

The truth may surprise you.

In March of 2009, Edward C. Green, director of Harvard's AIDS Prevention Research Project, spoke with *Christianity Today*.

INTERVIEWER: Is Pope Benedict being criticized unfairly for his comments about HIV and condoms?

DR. GREEN: This is hard for a liberal like me to admit, but yes, it's unfair because in fact, the best evidence we have supports his comments — at least his major comments, the ones I have seen.

INTERVIEWER: What does the evidence show about the effectiveness of condom-use strategies in reducing HIV infection rates among large-scale populations?

DR. GREEN: It will be easiest if we confine our discussion to Africa, because that's where the pope is, and that is what he was talking about. There's no evidence at all that condoms have worked as a public health intervention intended to reduce HIV infections at the "level of population." This is a bit difficult to understand. It may well make sense for an individual to use condoms every time, or as often as possible, and he may well decrease his chances of catching HIV. But we are talking about programs, large efforts that either work or fail at the level of countries, or, as we say in public health, the level of population. Major articles published in Science, The Lancet, British Medical Journal, and even Studies in Family Planning have reported this finding since 2004. I first wrote about putting emphasis on fidelity instead of condoms in Africa in 1988.[11]

In other words, the Church's position *saves lives*.

NOTES AND REFERENCES

[1] *Deliver Us From Evil*, Written and directed by Amy Berg, Disarming Films / Lions Gate Entertainment, 2006.

[2] See http://www.rottentomatoes.com/m/deliver_us_from_evil/?name_order=asc

[3] Shane Hickey and John Walshe, "Uproar as school footage used in film on paedophile," *The Independent* (Ireland), October 13, 2006.

[4] Ibid.

[5] Ibid.

[6] Grant Gallicho, "'Deliver Us From Evil' one-sided film about clergy sex abuse," Religion News Service, November 2006.

[7] "It's Time for Reporters to Seek Out the Facts About O'Grady Film," la-clergycases.com, October 12, 2006. Downloaded from bishop-accountability.org in October 2006.

[8] John Jay College of Criminal Justice, "The Nature and Scope of the Problem of Sexual Abuse of Minors by Catholic Priests and Deacons in the United States," 2004.

[9] Information complied from "Archdiocese of Los Angeles: Accused," posted at http://www.bishop-accountability.org/usccb/natureandscope/dioceses/reports/losangelesca-rpt-list.pdf

[10] Gallicho.

[11] Interview by Timothy C. Morgan, "Condoms, HIV, and Pope Benedict," *Christianity Today*, March 20, 2009.

Roman Polanski: Not a Catholic Priest

"[Roman Polanski's] soft deal was also in tune with the more permissive times, when sex with the under age was often winked at, especially among entertainment world sophisticates.

"'The sort of thing that would get guys arrested now was very common back then,' said [author] Michael Walker …

"Mr. Polanski was treated by the authorities … not so much as a sexual assailant but as someone in the mold of Isaac Davis, Mr. Allen's character from the movie *Manhattan*: that is, as a normally responsible person who had shown terrible judgment by having sex with a very young, but sophisticated, girl." – *New York Times*, October 11, 2009.[1]

By the late 1970's, Roman Polanski was one of Hollywood's most notable figures. A child survivor of the Holocaust, Polanski excelled to receive numerous Academy Award nominations for his directorial prowess. *Rosemary's Baby* and *Chinatown* are two of his most notable films.

In March of 1977, Los Angeles law enforcement arrested Polanski for the rape of a 13-year-old girl that occurred at the home of his friend, Jack Nicholson. Court records show that Polanski plied the underage girl with alcohol and drugged her. He then forcibly performed oral sex, intercourse, and sodomy.[2]

Polanski's legal team reached a plea bargain in which he was ordered to undergo a 90-day psychiatric evaluation in prison. Polanski was released from jail after serving just 42 days.

Polanski's lawyers believed that following his evaluation the director would simply be sentenced to probation. But soon they got wind that the judge in the case had bigger ideas. The jurist would allow Polanski to complete the 48 days remaining on his 90-day term if he would volunteer to be deported.

Such a light sentence for drugging and raping a 13-year-old would be unthinkable today. But this was 1977, and Polanski thought the punishment was too much.

He fled to France.

As the years passed, however, the inconvenience of not being able to travel to the United States and several other countries did not hinder Polanski from flourishing in Hollywood. His 1979 film *Tess* won three Oscars. For his 2002 film *The Pianist*, Polanski won the Academy Award for Best Director.

In the meantime, Polanski at times was publicly unapologetic for the rape he committed. In 1979, he told interviewer Martin Amis, "If I had killed somebody, it wouldn't have had so much appeal to the press, you see? But f---ing, you see, and the young girls. Judges want to f--

- young girls. Juries want to f--- young girls. Everyone wants to f--- young girls!"[3]

One would think that maybe a voice or two in the media would rightfully complain that Hollywood was "enabling" a child molester or condoning child rape. But throughout the 1980's and 90's, there was nary a voice critical of Polanski.

It was only after 2002, when the media began harping on the abuse by Catholic Church clergy, that a few people began to voice their demand for justice against the fugitive Polanski.

Defenders of Polanski continued to carry the day, however. In 2008, the HBO cable network presented *Roman Polanski: Wanted and Desired*,[4] a forceful presentation built around the premise that the judge in the Polanski case unfairly punished the Hollywood hero. The film argued that the jurist was publicity-hungry and had a "vindictive streak" against the director.

In September 2009, Polanski tried to travel to Switzerland to receive a Lifetime Achievement Award at the Zurich Film Festival, but he was seized at Zurich Airport on a 2005 international warrant for his arrest.

Several high-profile media figures ran to Polanski's defense. Woody Allen, Martin Scorsese, and Debra Winger were reportedly among the list of over 100 Hollywood figures who demanded Polanski's release. On a CNN interview, Tom O'Neill, senior editor of the celebrity magazine *In Touch Weekly*, cried, "It's mind boggling why they're still pursuing this ... It just seems that the prosecutors in Los Angeles won't let go these many years later."[5]

On the nationally syndicated television show *The View*, co-host Whoopi Goldberg downplayed Polanski's crime. "It wasn't rape-rape," she claimed. "We're (the United States) a different kind of society. We see things differently. The world sees 13 year olds and 14 year olds – in the rest of Europe, they are seen, often times [as adults]."[6]

Tom Shales, television critic for the *Washington Post*, opined, "[I]t may sound like a hollow defense, but in Hollywood I am not sure a 13-year-old is really a 13-year-old."[7]

Think about those remarks. Would these flimsy excuses ever be applied to defend an abusive Catholic priest? Of course not. It's impossible to imagine a pundit on national television pondering why folks just "won't let go" of decades-old cases of clergy abuse. And you'd never hear an international celebrity defending a priest by saying, "It wasn't rape-rape" or "A 13-year-old is not really a 13-year-old in (name your city here)."

Indeed, there were a few voices who demanded that Polanski face justice. Yet a few months after his arrest in Switzerland in 2009, in March of 2010, Polanski released his next film, *The Ghost Writer*. The *Los Angeles Times* dubbed it, "[A] dark pearl of a movie whose great flair and precision make it Polanski's best work in quite a while."[8] The *Times*' Kenneth Turan then concluded his review with the hope, "[W]ith any kind of luck this film just might signal a new beginning for Polanski."[9] Meanwhile, the *New York Times* called it a "very fine film from welcome start to finish."[10] The Berlin Film Festival awarded Polanski its best director award.

If not for simple anti-Catholicism, why is Roman Polanski feted by the Hollywood community when only a few miles away Cardinal Roger Mahony is excoriated?

In July of 2010, Swiss authorities announced that they would *not* be extraditing Polanski to the United States.

Roman Polanski: Not a Catholic Priest

If Roman Polanski were *Father* Roman Polanski, a Catholic priest who drugged and raped a 13-year-old, is there any doubt that authorities would have already extradited him years ago?[11]

"Turn over the files"?

In June of 2010, the *Los Angeles Times*' Steve Lopez, a perpetual critic of the Church, began an article, "I've said many times that Cardinal Roger Mahony should stop resisting the release of church documents in the sex abuse scandal."[12]

The problem? Cardinal Mahony already handed over the documents *years earlier*.

In the clergy abuse narrative, a continuing theme in the media and among victims groups is that the Church should "turn over all of their files." Unfortunately, it's not as simple as it sounds.

In a high-profile episode in the early 2000's, Cardinal Mahony resisted a demand to turn over personnel files of accused priests. The common explanation was that he did not want to release the files because they contained "damaging information" that would embarrass the Church and the Cardinal. This was *not* the reason. The reason was out of concerns for privacy laws.[13]

It's interesting. With the rise of the Internet, people are more concerned than ever about their privacy and personal information. In response to this, legislatures have acted accordingly, passing privacy laws to protect individuals. Yet these legalities and concerns about privacy seem to be forgotten when journalists and lawyers scream that the Church should "release their files."

Many prelates have been concerned that accused priests could sue them for violation of privacy. They would then have to pay substantial damages to individuals who may have abused children.

Indeed, the Diocese of Orange (CA) had to pay $100,000 to an admitted molester after the man filed a suit for violation of privacy.[14] Diocese lawyers begrudgingly acknowledged that during the course of his case information about the molester became public that shouldn't have. $100,000 ... to ... a ... molester. Cardinal Mahony surely did not want something like this to happen under his watch.

This was the *real* reason behind Cardinal Mahony (at the advice of his counsel) did not simply hand over priests' personnel files when asked.

The archdiocese was sued to release their files, and the case went to the Supreme Court. The Court, however, refused to hear the case, essentially dealing the archdiocese a loss.

What was the result of this? The archdiocese turned over the files. They have been in the hands of a judge for years.[15] Los Angeles attorneys have endlessly combed through them looking for something – *anything* – that could be the basis for a criminal case.

Years later, the files that everyone once screamed about have uncovered nothing.

In fact, in June of 2010, Los Angeles District Attorney Steve Cooley announced that after a very aggressive eight-year investigation, there was no evidence to bring any criminal charges against Los Angeles Church officials.

Roman Polanski: Not a Catholic Priest

NOTES AND REFERENCES

[1] Michael Cieply, "In Polanski Case, '70s Culture Collides With Today," *New York Times*, October 10, 2009, A1.

[2] Transcripts of grand jury testimonies, which include descriptions of the awful crime, are posted at "The Smoking Gun" web site. http://www.thesmokinggun.com/archive/polanskicover1.html

[3] L. Brent Bozell, "Hollywood's Favorite Rapist," Media Research Center, http://www.mrc.org/bozellcolumns/columns/2009/20091001123552.aspx, October 1, 2009.

[4] *Roman Polanski: Wanted and Desired*, Directed by Marina Zenovich, ThinkFilm / HBO, June 2008.

[5] Carolyn Plocher, "In Touch Weekly Senior Editor on Polanski Rape Case: 'It's Mind Boggling Why They're Still Pursuing This'," NewsBusters, http://newsbusters.org/blogs/carolyn-plocher/2009/09/28/touch-weekly-senior-editor-polanski-rape-case-it-s-mind-boggling-wh , September 28, 2008.

[6] Lachlan Markay, "The View's Whoopi Goldberg on Polanski: 'It Wasn't Rape-Rape'," NewsBusters, http://newsbusters.org/blogs/lachlan-markay/2009/09/29/views-whoopi-goldberg-polanski-it-wasnt-rape-rape#ixzz0u8hxhDhU , September 29, 2009.

[7] Mark Finkelstein, "Shales Defends Polanski: Hollywood 13-Yr. Olds Are Different," NewsBusters, http://newsbusters.org/blogs/mark-finkelstein/2009/10/06/shales-defends-polanski-hollywood-13-yr-olds-are-different#ixzz0u8iQCrb2 , October 6, 2009.

[8] Kenneth Turan, "Review: Roman Polanski's 'The Ghost Writer'," *Los Angeles Times*, February 19, 2010.

[9] Ibid.

[10] Manohla Dargis, "Writer for Hire Is a Wanted Man," *New York Times*, February 19, 2010.

[11] That "Father Polanski" would receive different treatment has also been put forth by other observers, including: Thomas J. Reese, S.J., "Father Polanski Would Go to Jail," WashingtonPost.com, September 28, 2009 and David Gibson, "Roman Polanski: What if He Were 'Father Polanski'?" PoliticsDaily.com, September 29, 2009.

[12] Steve Lopez, "Deposition paints an unflattering portrait of Mahony," *Los Angeles Times*, June 20, 2010.

[13] "LA Archdiocese Settles 45 Abuse Cases, 500 More to Go," *Which Way, LA?* (radio show / interview), KCRW 89.9 FM, host Warren Olney, December 6, 2006.

[14] Gustavo Arellano, "OC Diocese Paid Admitted Child Molester $100,000," *OC Weekly*, September 17, 2007. http://blogs.ocweekly.com/navelgazing/ex-cathedra/oc-diocese-paid-admitted-child/

[15] Tim Rutten, "L.A. has more serious things to worry about than Billy and the cardinal," *Los Angeles Times*, January 31, 2009.

18

Silent Ambassadors

"When people wish to destroy religion, they begin by attacking the priest, because where there is no longer any priest there is no sacrifice, and where there is no longer any sacrifice there is no religion." – St. John Vianney, Patron Saint of Parish Priests (1786-1859)[1]

Even back in the 19th century, when attacks on religion accentuated, St. Vianney could see that attacks on the Catholic faith begin with attacks on priests.

Again, the fact that priests harmed children is a binding fact that can never be negated. It is a deep shame that has tarnished the Church. It is a dark legend that the institution will forever live with.

However, judging from the writings of journalists and the actions of advocacy groups like SNAP, it's hard not to ignore that there is another agenda at play beyond the healing of victims and the protection of children.

In June of 2010, more than 10,000 Catholic priests and thousands of more followers descended upon Vatican City to mark the end of The Year for Priests. A year earlier,

DOUBLE STANDARD

Pope Benedict XVI had declared that the next twelve months would be dedicated to recognition and prayer for all Catholic priests and the extraordinary work that they do.

Indeed, contrary to what many may believe, the life of a common priest is quite stressful, laborious, and sacrificing. The length of the work week of a typical priest far exceeds that of most individuals. On a standard day, a priest rises early for prayer. Then he usually presides a morning Mass. What often follows are visits to the sick and infirmed. He may check in at a local homeless shelter or food bank. He may meet with a family who is suffering or enduring a difficult time. He may have to lead a funeral Mass. Then there may be meetings with couples who wish to get married in his parish. He meets with the budget manager to discuss the parish finances and problems. ("How do we pay to fix that annoying hum in the church's sound system?" "The air conditioner in the parish hall is broken." "Someone defaced the baptismal font.")

There are phone calls to return. There is mail and e-mail to open. There are invitations to attend local civic events. There are complaints to attend to. A young parishioner asks for a letter of recommendation. There are unannounced visits which may be important. An unexpected visitor desperately wants to give a confession. The secretary needs his signature so the office doesn't run out of paper. Maybe he meets with his local bishop. He may meet with the liturgy and music directors to coordinate special Masses. There are baptisms to prepare. There are the First Communion, Confirmation, and RCIA[2] classes to attend to. There are sessions for new extraordinary ministers and lectors. Maybe the annual church fair is approaching, help is lacking, and he needs to recruit volunteers. If the church has an accompanying school, there are visits to make there. Maybe he needs to meet with the school principal.

At the end of the day, a quiet dinner with some prayer is often a luxury.

Then there is always the homily for the approaching Sunday. For that there is often hours of preparation. One priest in England has said, "For each 60 seconds of preaching I reckon I need to spend 1 hour of preparation. I normally preach for 8-10 minutes."[3] Do the math, and the time piles up.

And there is one important characteristic about priests that is all too often forgotten. A priest is a member of a family like anyone else. He may have brothers and sisters. He may have nieces and nephews. There are parents and grandparents. Like any other private citizen, he experiences celebrations, trials, sadness, and responsibilities.

Priests are humans with emotions just like anyone else. They have personal interests and hobbies. They like sports, games, books, and movies. They have high-school buddies and friends from college.

Often in our culture today, if a celebrity does so much as write a modest check to a charity, an eager army of reporters and cameras will descend upon the scene to record the event to be broadcast across the country and published in newspapers and glossy magazines.

Meanwhile, an everyday priest gets no such recognition. If a newspaper, television station, or magazine recognizes a priest nowadays, it's most likely for a bad reason.

The last several years have been a tough time to be a priest. While nothing can compare with the profound and lasting pain of having been abused by a priest, surely the negative news of the past two decades has taken an emotional toll on those in the priesthood.

DOUBLE STANDARD

When Pope Benedict XVI formulated the Year for Priests, surely some of his consideration was for people to reflect on their local priests and recognize their hard work and sacrifices.

That is why it was particularly sad in June 2010 to see members of SNAP and members of the media go out of their way to make a scene at the closing of the end of the Year for Priests. Instead of allowing the Church a moment to celebrate its good and gracious priests, opponents of the faith reflexively seized an opportunity to holler about the Church's crimes and scream about celibacy and "women ordination." Peter Isely, the "Midwest Director" of SNAP, announced that he expected to hear an apology from the Pope for its handling of abuse cases.[4] Lost on the Isely and the media was the fact that the Holy Father had already apologized publicly on a number of occasions.

Before the end of the Year for Priests, Maureen Dowd, a high-profile columnist for the *New York Times*, ridiculed Catholic priests as "men in dresses."[5] As writer Charlotte Allen smartly noted, Dowd – or any other mainstream columnist – would never apply such a demeaning characterization to a Protestant minister, a Jewish rabbi, the Dalai Lama, or a man decked out like Marilyn Monroe in a gay pride parade.[6]

The double standard continues. The attacks on the priest and the Catholic Church persist.

Silent Ambassadors

NOTES AND REFERENCES

[1] St. John Vianney, "Catechism on the Priesthood," 1786-1859.

[2] RCIA is the "Rite of Christian Initiation of Adults," by which adults (usually) are introduced, then initiated, into the Catholic Church.

[3] "A day in the life of a priest," from http://www.catholicpriest.me.uk/dayinthelife.html Downloaded June 2010.

[4] Sylvia Poggioli, "Vatican Celebrations Overshadowed By Scandals," Vermont Public Radio, June 10, 2010.

[5] Maureen Dowd, "Worlds Without Women," *New York Times*, April 10, 2010.

[6] Charlotte Allen, "Undermining the faith," *Los Angeles Times*, May 2, 2010.

Index

ACORN, 85-87
AIDS/Africa, 137
Alinsky, Saul, 85-87, 88
Allen, Woody, 139, 141
Anderson, Jeff: *109-116*; 4; and ACLU, 115; and "Child Porn Initiative," 115-116; and SB 1779, 116-118; and SNAP 76, 77, 78
Applewhite, Dr. Monica, 48-49, 99-100
Associated Press 2007 study, 2, 16-17

Benedict XVI, Pope, 1, 78, 87-88
Berg, Amy, 129, 130, 133, 135, 136

Bernardin, Cardinal Joseph, 70-71
Blaine, Barbara, 77, 78, 89
Boston Globe, 16, 17, 22, 63, 72, 110
Boston Phoenix, 124
Boston, Archdiocese of, 63
Brewer, Adm. David L., 35-36
Brown, Bishop Tod David, 71
Brundage, Father Thomas, 3-4, 6*n*

Burton, Sen. John L., 117

CARA, 5*n*, 46
Carroll, Matt, 110
Casteix, Joelle, 94, 105
celibacy, 23, 97, 150
Charter for the Protection of Children and Young People, 96, 113-114

Chiampiou, Ken, 63

Christian Science Monitor, 16, 24

Christianity Today, 137
Clayton, Mark, 24
Clohessy, David: 77, 81; and ACORN, 85-87; and brother Kevin, 82-84
Clohessy, Kevin, 82-84
CNN, 11-12, 70, 141; and *Deliver Us From Evil*, 136

Cohan, Audrey, 8
Cooley, Steve, 144
Cortines, Ramon, 36
Daily Bulletin (CA), 19
de Souza, Father Raymond J., 4, 6*n*
Deady, Rev. John P., 55-56

153

Deliver Us From Evil (movie), 129-136
Department of Education (2004 study), 8, 15-16
Dober, Fr. Edward, 103-104, 105
Dolan, Archbishop Timothy, 87-88
Donohue, William, 25, 124
Dorris, Barbara, 97
Dowd, Maureen, 150
Doyle, Fr. Thomas, 130-131, 135-136
Drake, Tim, 47
Drivon, Laurence, 76, 117
Education Week, 9-10, 18
Eisenzimmer, Andrew, 48
FBI, 55, 103
Feldman, Charles, 36
Five Principles, 47, 114
Forbes, 76, 124
Gallegos, Mark, 53-55
Gallicho, Grant, 134, 135
Garabedian, Mitchell, 124
Geoghan, John, 123

George, Cardinal Francis, 111
Giuliani, Rudy, 89
Goldberg, Whoopi, 141
Good Morning America, 3

Goodman, Amy, 112
Goodstein, Laurie, 3-4
Green, Edward C., 137

Hare Krishnas, 2

Illinois, 20

Irish Bishops Conference (2009), 99-100
Isely, Peter, 150

Jenkins, Philip, 21-22
John & Ken Show, 62-63
John Jay study, 11, 45-46, 46, 133
John Paul II, Pope, 49

Ketchum, Katherine, 70
Kettelkamp, Teresa J., 47
Kobylt, John, 63
Koch, Edward "Ed", 4-5
Laugesen, Wayne, 5*n*
LAUSD, South East High, 29-31
Liberman, David, 2-3
Loftus, Dr. Elizabeth, 70-72
Lopez, Steve, 143
Los Angeles Unified School District (LAUSD), 20-21, *29-39*
Los Angeles Times, 16, 17, 20-21, 39, 71, 142, 143
Lyons, Daniel, 76, 124
MacLeish, Roderick Jr., 124
Maher, Joe, 59, 60, 62, 106, 111
Mahony, Cardinal Roger M., 64; and *Deliver Us From Evil*, 132-133, 134; measures taken, 93-95; 142; and privacy concerns, 143-144

Index

Manly, John C., 11, 64, 125, 131
Martini, Msgr. Richard, 104-105, 106
McHugh, Dr. Paul, 69
McNally, Dr. Richard, 69
McNamara, Eileen, 72
Murphy, Sean, 123-124, 125
NAMBLA, 115
National Catholic Register, 3, 47
National Review, 4
New Hamphire, 125-126
New York Post, 18, 21

New York Times, 3-5, 16, 17, 18, 24; 78-79; and Roman Polanski, 139, 142; 150

New York Times/CBS poll, 49
Newsweek, 23
Nussbaum, Martin, 48, 99
Ofshe, Richard, 69
O'Grady, Oliver, 129-136
Ohio, 19
O'Neill, Timothy P. Jr., 62
O'Neill, Tom, 141
Opus Bono Sacerdotii, 59-62
Ordinatio Sacerdotalis, 49-50
Oregonian, 20
Orthodox Jewish abuse, 24-25
Placa, Msgr. Alan, 89
Polanski, Roman, 139-143
Protestant abuse, 24
Rabinowitz, Dorothy, 123

repressed memories, 67-72

Rooney, Steve Thomas, 33-37
Sanchez-Ontiveros, Rev. Manuel, 53-56
SB 1179 (California Senate Bill), 117-119
Schiltz, Hon. Patrick J., 43-44
Schwada, John, 35
Seattle Times, 18, 19

Shakeshaft, Dr. Charol, 8, 15-16
Shales, Tom, 142
Shanley, Paul, 10
Silverglate, Harvey 124
SNAP: 7, and attack on Archbishop Dolan, 87-88; and BBB, 76; and Church teaching, 97; and Jeff Anderson 78; lawsuits, 89, 103-106; and lawyers, 76-78; and media, 78, 79; *New York Times* 78; and taxes, 76; 77-84, 94, 97, 105, 150
Time, 7
Vianney, St. John, 147
VIRTUS, 94, 96
Wall, Patrick, 131
Washington Post, 109, 142
Weigel, George, 43
Women "priests," 49
World Net Daily, 21
Worth, Byron, 123-124, 125
Year For Priests, 147, 150

Recommended by the Author

The scandals: Looking back and looking ahead

- Michael Rose, *Goodbye, Good Men* (Washington D.C.: Regnery Publishing, Inc., 2002) ... *Highly recommended*: What has gone so wrong in the Church the last 50 years? It started in the seminaries. This book will shock you. "[Rose] investigates how radical liberalism, like that found on many college campuses, has infiltrated the Catholic Church and tried to overthrow her traditional beliefs, standards, and disciplines – especially Church teachings on sexuality."

- George Weigel, *The Courage To Be Catholic: Crisis, Reform and the Future of the Church* (New York: Basic Books, 2002).

- Philip F. Lawler, *The Faithful Departed: The Collapse of Boston's Catholic Culture* (New York: Encounter Books, 2008).

- Tim Drake, "A Brief History of Abuse – And the Response To It," *National Catholic Register*, April 25-May 8, 2010 issue.

DOUBLE STANDARD

Catholicism

- *The Catechism of the Catholic Church* (New York: Doubleday, 1994) ... What the Church *really* teaches ... from the Church itself!

- *Ignatius Catholic Study Bible New Testament: RSV Second Catholic Edition* (Ignatius Press, 2010) ... Dr. Scott Hahn and Curtis Mitch. I love it!

- *The Essential Catholic Survival Guide: Answers to Tough Questions About the Faith* by The Staff at Catholic Answers (Catholic Answers, 2005) ... Do you have questions about what the Church *really* teaches? Do challenges to your faith leave you stumped? This easy-to-read reference is terrific.

- Anything by Peter Kreeft ... Author of over 40 books. A huge influence. *The Handbook of Christian Apologetics*, *Socrates Versus Marx*, *How to Win the Culture War*, *The Journey* ... many more.

- Anthony DeStefano, *Ten Prayers God Always Says Yes To* (New York: Doubleday, 2007).

Newspapers/Magazines

- *National Catholic Register* ... A gift every week. Simply great. ... www.ncregister.com

- *New Oxford Review* ... www.newoxfordreview.org

Recommended by the Author

- *This Rock* ... Catholic apologetics and evangelization ... http://www.catholic.com/magazines.asp

Internet

- www.catholic.com ... Catholic Answers: A fantastic resource for authentic Catholic information.

- www.catholicleague.org ... The Catholic League for Religious and Civil Rights: *The* organization combating anti-Catholicism in the U.S.

- www.catholicculture.org ... Catholic Culture: Smart, informative.

- www.catholicvoteaction.org ... CatholicVoteAction.org: Great Catholic voices.

- www.opusbono.org ... Opus Bono Sacerdotii ("Work for the Good of the Priesthood").

- www.newsbusters.org ... NewsBusters: A forum of the Media Research Center. I'm a contributing writer.

- www.themediareport.com ... TheMediaReport.com: My web site! "Examining anti-Catholicism and bias in the media."

DOUBLE STANDARD

Television and radio

- *EWTN* ... Television and radio. Thank you, Mother Angelica. My ride to work is much better with "The Son Rise Morning Show," hosted by Brian Patrick, on my Sirius satellite radio.

- *The Catholic Channel* ... On my Sirius satellite radio. I really appreciate "Seize the Day with Gus Lloyd."

- CatholicTV ... Fr. Robert Reed.

Made in the USA
Charleston, SC
08 April 2011